While Waiting

George E. Verrilli, M.D., F.A.C.O.G.
Anne Marie Mueser, Ed.D.

St. Martin's Griffin
New York

Editor: Barbara Anderson
Design: Michael Mendelsohn and Alex Soma of Harry Chester, Inc.
Illustrations on pages 77, 81, 82, 86, 90, 92, 95, 96, 104, 106, 107, 108, 111, 115, and 116 by Durell Godfrey.
Illustrations on pages 8, 10, 11, 12, 13, 14, 15, 16, and 17: Kristina Nörgaard
Illustrations on pages 54, 69, 70, 71, 72, 73, 74, and 123: George Wildman

"Welcome Baby" designed by Harry Chester Associates, copyright © 1981 by George Verrilli and Anne Marie Mueser.

Library of Congress Cataloging-in-Publication Data

Verrilli, George E.
　　While waiting/George E. Verrilli and Anne Marie Mueser.—Rev.
　ed.
　　　　p.　　cm.
　　Includes bibliographical references and index.
　　ISBN 0-312-09938-X
　　1. Pregnancy.　2. Childbirth.　3. Prenatal care.　4. Pregnancy.
　5. Childbirth.　6. Prenatal care.　I. Mueser, Anne Marie.
　II. Title.
　RG525.V45　1993
　618.2'4—dc20　　　　　　　　　　　　　　　　　93–26698
　　　　　　　　　　　　　　　　　　　　　　　　　　CIP

PUBLISHING HISTORY

- Originally published as *While Waiting: A Prenatal Guidebook* in 1982 by St. Martin's Press.
- Updated versions of original edition published in 1984, 1985, 1986, 1987, and 1989.
- More than 3 million copies of original edition in print through 30 printings.
- First printing of fully revised edition published November 1993.

First St. Martin's Griffin Edition: November 1993.

10　9　8　7　6　5　4　3

CONTENTS

ON THE COVER

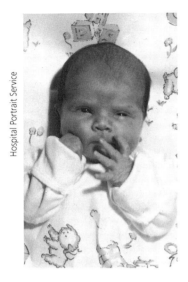

Ánna Máire Mueser—delivered by Dr. Verrilli—arrived on August 13, 1980, at 3:07 P.M. She weighed 6 pounds, 6 ounces and was 18 inches in length. The cover picture was taken a day later by a member of the Mother's Club of Northern Dutchess Hospital, under contract with Hospital Portrait Service.

Note the shape of Ánna Máire's head, the slightly swollen eyelids, the wrinkled skin on her hands, and the way one hand is curled into a little fist. These are all typical characteristics of a newborn.

ACKNOWLEDGMENTS

Many people have contributed to the ongoing success of *While Waiting*. As this new edition goes to press, the authors especially wish to thank:

- our editor, Barbara Anderson, for her patience, competence, and never-ending support through the years, and her assistant, Marian Lizzi, who remained cheerful and helpful while choreographing many needed steps to bring this revision to press;

- Barbara M. Perkins, Cecelia Worth, and all the others who contributed to the original edition, and everyone at Harry Chester, Incorporated, who once again made the pages happen;

- the administration and staff at Northern Dutchess Hospital and Hudson Valley Associates who provide a supportive atmosphere for family-centered childbirth, and the many care providers and more than three million women and their partners who have used *While Waiting;*

- Chris Verrilli, mother of Bianca, Ariana, and Gregory, for her encouragement and support;

- Andrea Greaney, whose waiting for Michael, Steven, and John went almost by the book, for her page-by-page efforts; and

- our cover girl, Ánna Máire, and her father, whose contribution is beyond measure.

NOTE TO THE READER

It is important that every pregnant woman obtain appropriate professional prenatal care. Any reader who experiences any of the warning signs or symptoms mentioned in this book should seek prompt and appropriate professional care.

The suggestions and other information in this book are intended for use in consultation with your health-care providers. Neither this nor any other book should be used as a substitute for professional prenatal care of for medical care or treatment.

INTRODUCTION _____

While Waiting contains many of the things I discuss with women who come to my office for prenatal care. Annie Mueser, who listened to most of what I told her while she was pregnant, has drawn on her many years of experience as a writer and teacher to put this information in its present form.

The material in this fully revised and updated edition includes topics suggested by some of the more than three million women and their care providers who used *While Waiting* in its first decade. The book is designed for easy reference. In the sections "Coping with Bodily Changes" and "For Your Information," topics are arranged alphabetically so you can quickly locate what you need. You don't have to sit down and read the entire book from cover to cover, although we hope you'll do that too.

We suggest that you use this book as if you were having a conversation with your prenatal care provider. Bring it to your appointments, and if you have questions about anything you've read, be sure to ask. Your health-care team, of course, knows you personally and may modify some of the suggestions to fit your particular situation.

And, you should remember that professionals may differ in their opinions regarding certain of these matters. Our guidelines are offered as suggestions, not absolutes. Use the information here to help you work with your prenatal care provider. The book contains pages to keep track of your appointments, diet, questions, and other important items as your pregnancy progresses. We hope you'll find this material useful while waiting.

George E. Verrilli, M.D.

SECTION ONE

WORKING WITH YOUR CARE PROVIDER

FIRST PRENATAL VISIT

Personal History
Physical Exam
Prenatal Laboratory Tests

WHEN IS YOUR BABY DUE?

FOLLOW-UP VISITS

BETWEEN VISITS

IMPORTANT WARNING SIGNS

APPOINTMENT RECORD

QUESTIONS AND NOTES

HOW YOUR BABY GROWS

SOME QUESTIONS . . . WHILE WAITING

If you are pregnant, you probably are already going to the caregiver of your choice for prenatal care. If you have not yet chosen a prenatal care provider—physician, midwife, clinic—we suggest that you do so as soon as possible.

FIRST PRENATAL VISIT _____

Most prenatal care providers welcome both parents at visits to the office. You may, of course, go to your appointments by yourself, or you may wish to bring another person close to you with a special interest in your pregnancy. Feel free to ask any questions you have about this.

The first prenatal visit is designed to gain a picture of your general condition going into this pregnancy, and to make sure your care provider has the necessary information to work with you in the way that will be best for you and your baby.

PERSONAL HISTORY

You will be asked to provide facts about your health and the health of your baby's father. Hereditary possibilities (twins, for example, or a family history of certain diseases) will be discussed.

You will be asked about your gynecological and obstetrical history—any conditions that might affect your reproductive health or comfort (for example, difficulty with your menstrual periods, pelvic inflammatory disease, sexually transmitted diseases, urinary tract infections) and previous pregnancies, if any (including miscarriages or abortions).

You will be asked questions about your general health, and especially about conditions such as hypertension, diabetes, heart disease, kidney problems, or any others that might affect the medical management of your pregnancy.

Your care provider will ask you specific questions about this pregnancy. When was your last menstrual period? What signs of pregnancy have you already noticed? Did you use a home pregnancy test to confirm your pregnancy?

Questions about your work and life-style, including your nutritional and exercise patterns, will help identify potential risk factors and circumstances for which you may need special support.

It's important to answer the questions as completely as you can, even if there are details you think may be unimportant or would prefer to forget. The interview will probably be a bit longer if you are visiting a care provider for the first time.

Even if you and your caregiver have worked together previously, you should feel free to revisit any information you believe may be relevant. Don't be afraid to ask questions—old or new—or to discuss any recent changes in your life and expectations for your care that may not be reflected in your file.

PHYSICAL EXAM

The physical examination at your first prenatal visit will include a careful assessment of your breasts, throat, lungs, kidneys, liver, heart and blood pressure, bladder, uterus, and birth canal in regard to your developing pregnancy. The internal pelvic evaluation will check for any structural or other conditions that might affect your pregnancy, labor, and delivery. You will be weighed.

PRENATAL LABORATORY TESTS

At your first prenatal visit, a number of laboratory tests will be done to obtain information to monitor your health and that of your developing baby. These tests are likely to include:

- A urine specimen that will be tested for the presence of protein, glucose (sugar), and perhaps nitrites, bilirubin, and/or ketones, to keep track of kidney function. A bacterial analysis to check for infection also may be done, and treatment will be prescribed if needed.

- A Pap smear (unless you have had one done within the past year) to screen for cervical cancer.

- A blood sample will be taken and tested for a number of different things:
  —Your blood type and whether or not you carry the Rh factor (see page 105).
  —Red blood cell level (hematocrit, or hemoglobin) to see if you and your baby are getting enough oxygen.
  —Whether or not you carry antibodies to rubella (German measles) (see page 105).
  —Presence of syphilis (this test may be required by law in some states) (see page 106).

- A culture to detect the presence of gonorrhea, and one to check for chlamydia (see page 85).

- Any other tests that might be specifically indicated for your particular circumstances, at your request or the suggestion of your care provider. (Such tests might include a blood test to check for Lyme disease [see page 98] or the presence of the HIV virus [see page 78].)

WHEN IS YOUR BABY DUE? _____

There is a formula for estimating this date, but keep in mind that it is only an estimate. It is quite normal for a baby to be born as much as two weeks before or after this date. Your body and your baby will decide the right time. At your first prenatal visit, your care provider will help you estimate and note this date. As time goes on, if your pregnancy seems to be developing in a way significantly inconsistent with the estimated due date, a sonogram (see pages 112–3) may be suggested to obtain additional information.

To estimate the due date, add seven days to the first day of your last menstrual period. Then count back three months.

An average pregnancy is 280 days, or 40 weeks from the first day of the last menstrual period if your cycle is regular. If figured from the time of ovulation, an average pregnancy is 266 days. You can add or subtract one day for each day that your menstrual cycle is longer or shorter than the average length of twenty-eight days.

Later in your pregnancy, another way to estimate your baby's due date is to add five months to the time you first feel fetal movement.

FOLLOW-UP VISITS

For a woman without any special risk factors, a typical schedule of prenatal care visits is likely to include an appointment once each month until about the 28th week (the beginning of the third trimester), an appointment every other week for the next two months, and weekly visits in the last month, until delivery.

The schedule of your prenatal care visits may vary from the norm and will depend on any special circumstances or risk factors in your case.

During each prenatal care visit, your care provider will discuss with you the progress of your pregnancy and any problems you might have. Bring any questions you have with you, and don't be afraid to ask.

A number of routine items will be checked and noted during each regular visit to your prenatal care provider:

- You will be weighed.
- Your blood pressure will be checked.
- Your caregiver will listen to the fetal heartbeat. (The device used may let you listen, too.)
- Your abdomen will be examined to note the size of your growing uterus.
- Your urine will be checked for protein and glucose and, if indicated, other substances. Your caregiver may give you a container and have you provide the sample at the time of your office visit. If you are asked to bring a urine sample, bring with you the first urine of the morning in a clean container. If your appointment is later in the day, refrigerate the sample if possible.
- You will be examined for signs of excessive fluid retention. Although some edema (swelling) is normal, too much may indicate a developing problem.

From time to time during the course of your pregnancy, additional observations and tests may be suggested. What is recommended for you will, of course, depend on the particular circumstances of your pregnancy. These tests may include one or more of the following:

- An alpha fetoprotein (AFP) test (see page 79).
- Ultrasound (see pages 112–13).
- Amniocentesis or Chorionic Villus Sampling (see pages 80 and 85–6).
- Tests for maternal infections such as group B streptococcus and/or hepatitis B.
- A glucose challenge test (GCT) to check for gestational diabetes (see pages 94–5), with a follow-up glucose tolerance test (GTT) if indicated.

If you have questions about what is or is not being recommended for you, or you have questions about the findings, feel free to ask.

During the ninth month, your office visits will include preparation for labor and delivery and an internal examination to check the condition of your cervix (effacement and dilation), the baby's position relative to your pelvic opening (station), and the baby's presenting part (see pages 123–4). If you have any questions about what this means, ask.

BETWEEN VISITS

If you have any problems of a medical nature—for example, fever, chills, bladder or bowel difficulties, sore throat or cold, bleeding, dizziness, spots before your eyes, tingling or numbness—call your prenatal care provider.

If you should require medication, you must take one that is safe during pregnancy. You should check with your prenatal care provider before taking any medication while you are pregnant—even something you've routinely taken in the past or a medication prescribed by a physician who is not your prenatal caregiver (see pages 76–7, 87, 100–1, and 104–5).

To keep you and your baby healthy, it's important that you and your prenatal care provider work together.

IMPORTANT WARNING SIGNS

Any of the following may be a warning that you need medical help. Call your prenatal care provider without delay if you experience any of these symptoms:

- severe or persistent headache
- blurred vision or spots before your eyes
- severe abdominal pain or cramps, perhaps with nausea or diarrhea
- severe or persistent vomiting
- severe, unexplained pain in the shoulder
- high fever (above 101°F.)
- marked swelling in your upper body (face or hands)
- a sudden weight gain in just a few days
- vaginal bleeding
- gush or flow of watery fluid from your vagina
- marked decrease in output of urine
- regular contractions, getting stronger as time progresses
- marked decrease or stopping of fetal movement you feel (from the fifth month on)

Do not hesitate to call your care provider even if you fear you may be overreacting to something that might turn out to be unimportant. It's better to be safe than sorry.

APPOINTMENT RECORD

Date	Time	Weight	Blood Pressure	Urine	Other

QUESTIONS AND NOTES

HOW YOUR BABY GROWS _____

The following pages contain a brief, month-by-month description of the characteristics of a developing baby. The information offered here is based on average development. Although no two pregnancies are exactly alike, it will give you some idea of the nature and sequence of changes going on within your body.

Each page provides a place for your own notes as your pregnancy progresses. Use this space, if you wish, to jot down things that matter to you personally. You can keep track of your pregnancy's important milestones—for example, the first time you feel your baby move or when you first notice Braxton-Hicks contractions (see pages 24–5 and 124). If the perfect name for your baby comes to mind, write it down. Describe any experiences, thoughts, or feelings you want to be sure to remember later. These are your pages. Use them as you choose.

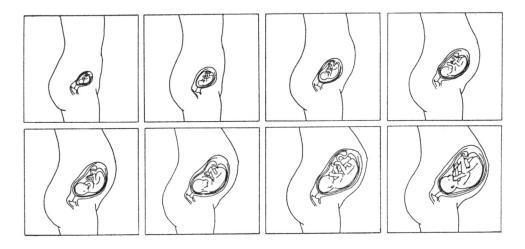

THE FIRST TRIMESTER _____

THE FIRST TWO WEEKS

Your baby's life and growth begin at the moment a sperm joins the ripe ovum (egg) in one of your fallopian tubes. These two cells fuse and become one. The cell formed by the united sperm and egg—although it is no larger than the dot at the end of this sentence—contains the potential for everything your baby will become.

Within about half an hour, the cell formed by the joined sperm and ovum divides into two cells. The cells continue to divide as they travel toward the uterus. By the end of the first week to ten days, the cluster of cells completes its journey down the fallopian tube and attaches to the uterine wall.

The cells continue to divide at a very rapid rate. Those that will become the placenta grow against the uterine wall. The placenta connects to the little developing form by the umbilical cord. The cord brings nourishment from your body to your baby while carrying off wastes from the baby so that your body can dispose of them.

THIRD AND FOURTH WEEKS

Even before you may know for sure that you are pregnant, your baby's central nervous system, heart, and lungs start to develop. The tiny heart begins to beat.

By the end of the fourth week, the baby is about 3/16 of an inch long. Although distinct facial features are not yet apparent, the face is beginning to form and dark circles mark where the eyes will be.

SECOND MONTH

As the second month begins, your baby's ears are starting to develop. Each ear begins as a little fold of skin at the side of the head. Tiny buds that eventually will grow into arms and legs are forming. By this time, the brain and the spinal cord are already well formed. The head is large in proportion to the rest of the body.

At the end of eight weeks, your baby is about an inch long and weighs about 1/30 of an ounce. Now the arms and legs are beginning to show distinct divisions, including fingers and toes. The little buds that will become fingers already have fingerprints.

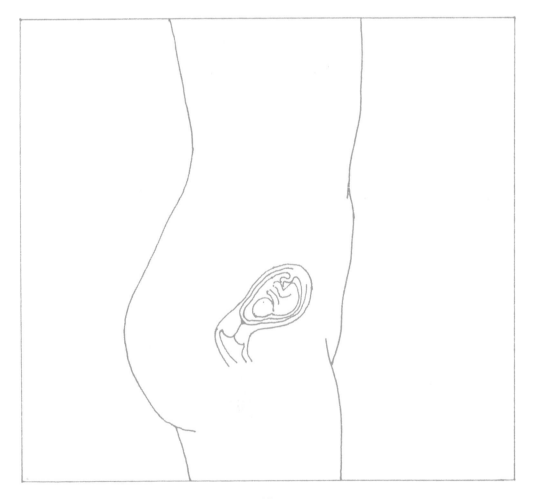

THIRD MONTH

By the end of three months, your baby is about three inches long and weighs about one ounce. The arms, with hands and fingers, and the feet, with toes, are fully formed. Fingernails and toenails are beginning to develop and the external ears are formed by this time. The beginnings of teeth are forming in the tiny jawbones.

The external sex organs are apparent by this time, and the internal sex organs are developing as well. If your baby is a boy, his testicles already contain sperm. If your baby is a girl, her ovaries already contain ova. So even before this baby is born, the promise of the future generation is already present in these tiny cells.

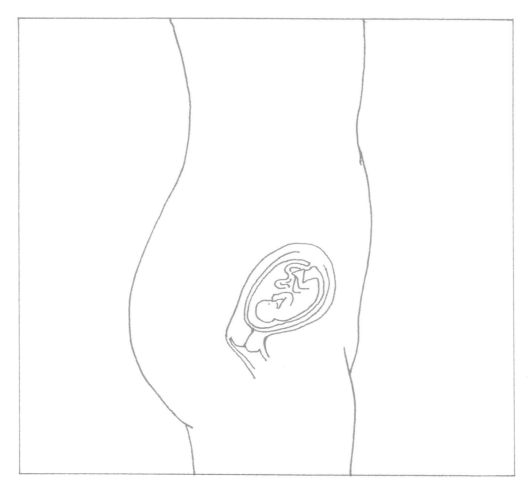

THE SECOND TRIMESTER _____

FOURTH MONTH

Your baby's heartbeat can now be heard using a special stethoscope. Compared to the rest of the body, your baby's head seems very large at this point. Your baby's length will increase rapidly during this month.

By the end of the fourth month, your baby is about seven inches long and weighs about four ounces. The baby already has eyebrows and lashes and can suck his or her thumb.

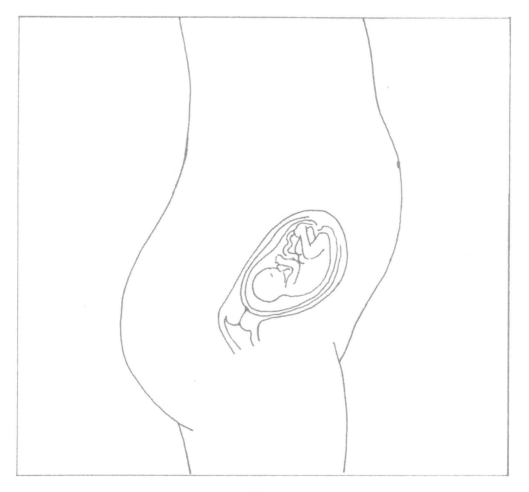

FIFTH MONTH

During the fifth month, your baby weighs from one-half to one pound and is about ten to twelve inches long. Your baby is busy developing muscles and exercising them. Although he or she has been moving for some time now, it's during this month that most mothers feel the baby move for the first time. The time when you begin to feel your baby move is called "quickening."

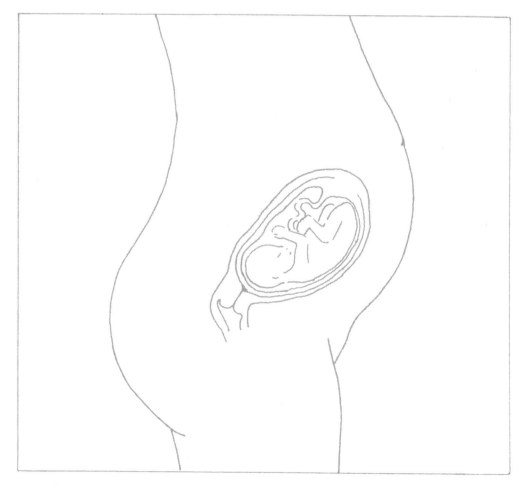

SIXTH MONTH

At the end of the sixth month, your baby measures eleven to fourteen inches long and may weigh as much as 1½ to 2 pounds. The skin is reddish in color, wrinkled, and covered with a heavy, protective, creamy coating called vernix caseosa.

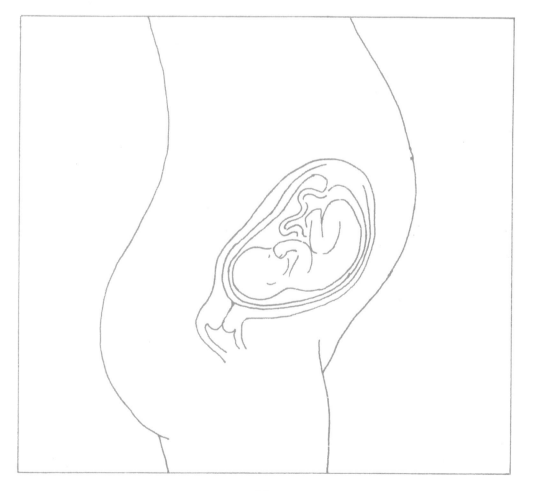

THE THIRD TRIMESTER _____

SEVENTH MONTH

During this month, your baby continues to grow and exercise. During the last part of the seventh month, a baby born prematurely has a chance for survival if skilled intensive care is provided.

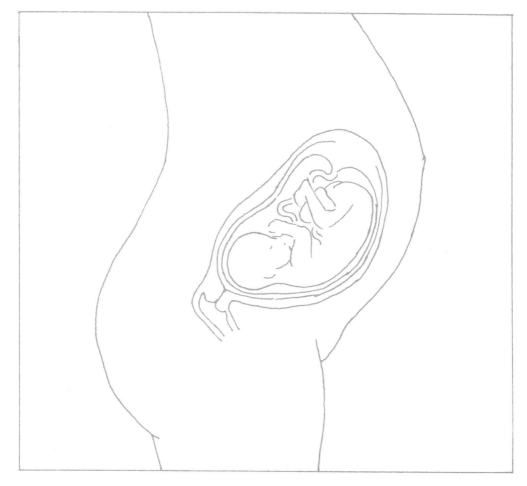

EIGHTH MONTH

Your baby is getting longer and fatter. He or she is now about eighteen inches long with a weight of as much as five pounds. If born prematurely at the end of the eighth month, a baby's chances for survival are good.

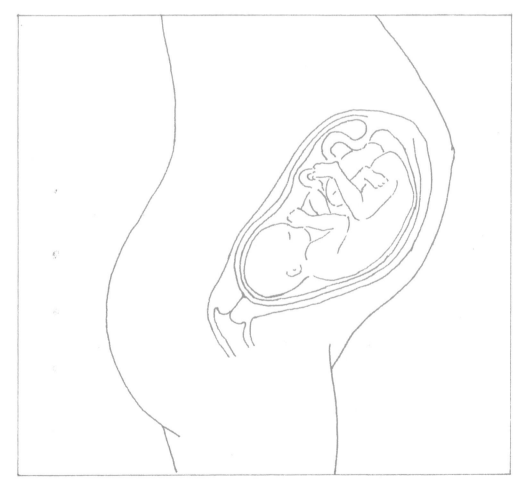

NINTH MONTH

During this month, your baby continues to grow and mature. At the end of the ninth month, an average full-term baby weighs 7 to 7½ pounds and is about twenty inches long. The skin is still coated with its creamy protective covering.

Sometime during the ninth month, your baby's position changes to get ready for labor and delivery. The baby drops down into your pelvis and the head engages in the birth position. Your baby is ready to be born.

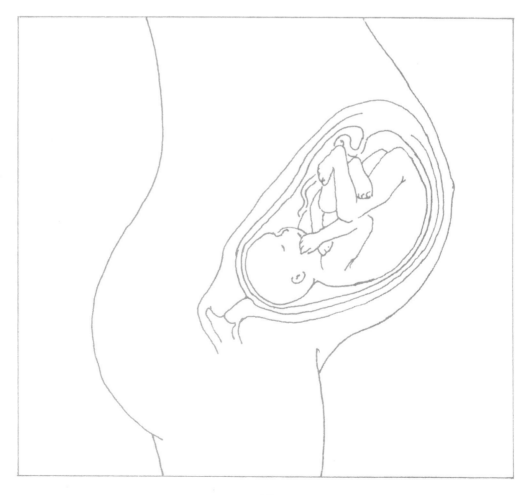

SOME QUESTIONS . . . WHILE WAITING _____

Many women have questions and concerns about prenatal care and about labor and delivery. This is especially likely for a first baby. You will find a discussion of a number of these topics in "For Your Information," beginning on page 75.

You should feel free to ask any questions you might have, and this list is designed to help you do that. Circle the ? next to each question you would like to discuss with your care provider. Mark with an X each question that has already been answered or is not of interest to you.

?	How can I tell if I am high risk? If I am, what should I be doing differently? What extra precautions will be taken by my care provider?
?	What special prenatal diagnostic tests, if any, will be suggested for me? Why? May I request a test if it would make me feel more secure? May I choose to refuse a suggested prenatal test?
?	What type of childbirth preparation classes should my partner and I attend? How soon must we make our plans?
?	What are the chances that I will need a Caesarean delivery? How can I prepare for this? If this happens, can my partner remain with me?
?	If I have previously had a Caesarean, will I be permitted to labor and attempt a vaginal delivery this time? What can I do to increase the chances of a successful vaginal birth after Caesarean (VBAC)?
?	If I prepare for an unmedicated delivery, do I have the option of changing my mind?
?	If I prefer not to be medicated, how can I ensure that the hospital staff will respect my wishes?

?	If I require medication during labor or delivery, what will be available to me? How will this affect the baby? How will it alter my birthing experience?
?	In preparing me for delivery, will an enema and/or pubic shave be ordered or suggested? If I choose not to have one or both of these procedures, how can this be arranged?
?	Will I be required to have an IV in place during labor as a matter of routine? In the absence of any special medical indications for an IV, may I choose to refuse this intervention?
?	If my membranes do not rupture spontaneously before or during early labor, will an amniotomy be required? If so, why? When might this be done? May I choose not to have this procedure?
?	Will my labor be monitored electronically on a continuous basis? What alternatives do I have if I choose not to be monitored in this way?
?	Who will be my birth attendants when the time comes? May I hire a monitrice (private obstetrical nurse) to attend me during my labor and delivery?
?	Will I be permitted to walk around during labor? May I labor in the shower or a warm tub bath if I wish to do so? Will I be encouraged to labor and deliver in the position I find most comfortable?
?	May I invite someone in addition to my support partner to be with me during labor and delivery? What about friends or my other children?
?	What is a forceps delivery? Why is this sometimes necessary? Would vacuum extraction be an available alternative if assistance were needed to get the baby through the birth canal?
?	Must an episiotomy be done as a matter of routine? What can we do to reduce the need for this procedure?

?	What arrangements, if any, must be made in advance for the Leboyer approach to a nonviolent birth?
?	If I plan to breastfeed my baby and need additional help or information, is there a local chapter of La Leche League volunteers or some other support group available in my area?
?	What is bonding? Are there any special preparations I should make for this? How much time will I be able to spend with my baby in the delivery room?
?	Will I be permitted to nurse my baby immediately after delivery if I wish?
?	What routine medical procedures will be required for my baby immediately after birth? May I choose to delay or modify these routines?
?	How can I choose a pediatrician or family-care physician who will support me in the early experiences I wish for my baby, my partner, and myself as a family?
?	If all goes well, how soon after my baby is born may we go home from the hospital or birth center?
?	
?	
?	

COPING WITH BODILY CHANGES

BACKACHE

BLADDER PROBLEMS

BREASTS (LEAKAGE)

BREASTS (SIZE AND APPEARANCE)

CONSTIPATION

CONTRACTIONS (DURING PREGNANCY)

FAINTNESS

GUMS (BLEEDING AND SWELLING)

HEADACHES

HEART POUNDING (PALPITATIONS)

HEARTBURN OR INDIGESTION

HEMORRHOIDS

LEG CRAMPS

NAUSEA AND VOMITING

NOSEBLEEDS

PELVIC PAIN OR DISCOMFORT

SALIVATION (EXCESSIVE)

SHORTNESS OF BREATH

SKIN
(BLOTCHES AND DISCOLORING)

STRETCH MARKS

SWELLING (FEET, LEGS, AND
HANDS)

TIREDNESS

VAGINAL DISCHARGE

VARICOSE VEINS

COPING WITH BODILY CHANGES

The following section describes some of the bodily changes that accompany pregnancy. Suggestions for coping comfortably with these changes are included. You may find some of these suggestions helpful. Remember, however, that no two pregnancies are exactly alike, and just because a particular problem is listed doesn't mean it will happen in your case. Few women will experience all of the discomforts mentioned, and you may avoid many or even most of them.

 most likely at this time   may occur at this time   least likely at this time

BACKACHE

WHEN

Mid-to-late pregnancy.

1	2	3	4	5	6	7	8	9

WHY

As your body's weight, shape, and balance change, you may alter the way you sit and stand. This can cause muscle strain. In late pregnancy, if the baby is facing front with the back of his or her head pressing against your sacrum, severe low backache may result.

TRY THIS

- Make an effort to maintain good posture.
- Use sensible body mechanics to avoid strain. For example, squat instead of bending over from the waist. Rise from lying down by rolling onto your side and pushing yourself up with your hands.
- Massage or gentle daily exercise may help, especially for the sore spots. Try head rolling and shoulder rotating for discomfort in the upper back. Pelvic rocking in the "angry cat" position should help the lower back (see pages 71 and 73).
- Wear comfortable shoes with heels of a height you are used to. This is not a time for very high heels or shoes so different from what you usually wear that your comfort and balance are affected.
- For a low backache caused by pressure of the baby, rest in a position that takes the baby's weight off your spine. Get down on all fours. Pretend you are scrubbing the floor on your hands and knees or, if you prefer, go ahead and actually do it. The position and type of movement involved may help ease the pain.

BLADDER PROBLEMS

WHEN

Throughout pregnancy, but especially during early and late pregnancy.

1	2	3	4	5	6	7	8	9

WHY

During the first trimester, your growing uterus and developing baby press against your bladder, causing a frequent need to urinate. This will happen again near the end of pregnancy, when the baby has dropped in preparation for being born. Hormones and the increased volume of your circulation also affect bladder control and the potential for urinary tract infections.

TRY THIS

- During pregnancy, frequent urination is normal. There's nothing you can do about it, so accept it and plan accordingly. Each time you use the toilet, try to empty your bladder as completely as you can.
- Drink plenty of liquids, especially water. Reducing your fluid intake does not solve the problem of needing to urinate often, and you need fluids to keep your kidneys functioning well.
- If your urine burns or stings, you may have a urinary tract infection. Consult your caregiver without delay, because such infections only get worse if left untreated. Continue to drink plenty of fluids. Cranberry juice may help.
- Cotton underpants, or at least those with a cotton crotch, are better than those made from synthetic fabrics. Avoid pants or pantyhose that fit tightly against the crotch.
- When you empty your bladder, you may find it soothing to rinse yourself with warm water. To minimize the chance of infection, always wipe from front to back.

BREASTS (LEAKAGE) _____

WHEN

Anytime from the fifth month on.

1	2	3	4	5	6	7	8	9

WHY

Your breasts produce colostrum, a yellowish or clear liquid, intended to be your baby's first food. Some women experience leakage of this fluid in late pregnancy. Others do not. Either condition is normal.

TRY THIS

- Tuck a cotton handkerchief or gauze pad into each bra cup to absorb leaking fluid. You can buy nursing pads made especially for this purpose in a pharmacy or health-and-beauty-aid store. Avoid plastic shields, which trap moisture and prevent air from circulating. Replace the pads when they get wet.
- If leaking colostrum dries and becomes crusty on your nipples, wash it off with plain warm water. Soap may dry or irritate your nipples.

BREASTS (SIZE AND APPEARANCE) _____

WHEN

Throughout pregnancy.

1	2	3	4	5	6	7	8	9

23

WHY

Your breasts will increase in size because your milk glands enlarge and there is an increase in fatty tissue. They may become tender and more sensitive. As your blood supply increases in volume and the blood vessels enlarge, bluish veins may appear.

TRY THIS

- Wear a bra that gives you firm support. This will ease the strain on breast tissue and also on your back muscles if your breasts are heavy.
- Choose cotton bras in preference to those made from synthetic fabric. Cotton allows the skin to breathe.
- As your size changes, make sure your bra size does, too. Your bra should fit well without binding or irritating your nipples. You may need a larger-size bra or a style that's cut differently. Try a maternity or a nursing bra if you can't find a regular one that fits well.

CONSTIPATION _____

WHEN

Mid- through late pregnancy.

1	2	3	4	5	6	7	8	9

WHY

During pregnancy, your growing uterus takes up part of the working space of your digestive system. Hormones, too, may slow intestinal movement. In some cases, iron and vitamin supplements may contribute to constipation.

TRY THIS

- Drink at least two quarts (8 to 10 glasses) of fluids daily. Try starting your day with a glass of fruit juice when you first get up in the morning.
- Eat raw vegetables, fruits, and whole grain cereals and bread daily to make sure you're getting enough fiber. Be sure to include prunes, dates, or figs in your diet.
- Try to give yourself time for a bowel movement at about the same time every day, or at least go when you have the urge. Don't put it off.
- Daily exercise may be helpful.
- Avoid mineral oil, which can remove vitamins A, D, and E from your body. If you feel that you need a laxative, consult your prenatal caregiver. Don't use a laxative, enema, or over-the-counter remedy on your own.
- Ask your prenatal caregiver if you should try a stool softener. Stool softeners, which act only in the digestive tract, are not irritating or habit forming.

CONTRACTIONS (DURING PREGNANCY) _____

WHEN

Possibly as early as the fourth month, although most women don't notice them until the seventh or eighth month.

1	2	3	4	5	6	7	8	9

WHY

Uterine muscles tighten irregularly from about the fourth week of pregnancy on. These contractions are called Braxton-Hicks contractions. They differ from the contractions of labor in that they don't get stronger as time progresses and they don't result in your baby's birth.

TRY THIS

- Continue your regular activities. Walking may be helpful.

- If you are uncomfortable, make a conscious effort to relax from head to toe. Understand and work with your body as it prepares in this normal way for labor and delivery.

- If contractions are severe or persistent, or if they seem to be getting stronger, consult your prenatal care provider.

FAINTNESS

WHEN

Early and late pregnancy.

1	2	3	4	5	6	7	8	9

WHY

If you stand for long periods of time, low blood pressure may cause faintness. This is especially likely to occur in warm, crowded places or during long, uncomfortable periods of inactivity, such as standing on line at a checkout counter. In late pregnancy, lying on your back may cause your blood pressure to drop and you may feel dizzy or faint when you first get up. Faintness may also result from low blood sugar or anemia (too little iron in the blood).

TRY THIS

- After the fourth month of pregnancy, be careful not to lie flat on your back. Sleep on your side or propped up on pillows. If you find you have rolled onto your back while sleeping, lie on your left side a few minutes before trying to get up.

- Try to avoid standing for long periods of time. If you must stand, move around frequently to stimulate your circulation. If you're on line or in a crowd where you can't go anywhere, shifting your weight back and forth from one leg to the other will help.

- To keep your blood sugar up and at a more even level, eat healthful foods in small amounts at frequent intervals throughout the day. Choose foods with complex carbohydrates (bread, pasta, fresh fruit and vegetables, cereal) rather than those laden with simple carbohydrates (sugar). (See pages 38–43, and 48.)

- If faintness is a recurring problem for you, be sure to mention it to your prenatal caregiver. If anemia is detected, changes in your diet will be recommended and supplementary iron may be prescribed (see pages 54–5).

GUMS (BLEEDING AND SWELLING) _____

WHEN

Mid- to late pregnancy.

1	2	3	4	5	6	7	8	9

WHY

During pregnancy, the increase in your volume of circulation and supply of certain hormones may cause tenderness, swelling, and bleeding of gums. A lack of vitamin C in your diet also may contribute to this condition.

TRY THIS

- Be sure you don't neglect proper care of your teeth and gums, even though discomfort may tempt you to ignore regular brushing and flossing.

- An antiseptic mouthwash such as Listerine keeps your mouth feeling fresh and may reduce the potential for gum infections. (Remember, you're supposed to swish it around and spit it out, not swallow it.)

- A professional cleaning of your teeth and gums early in pregnancy and perhaps again before you deliver is a good idea. If you routinely require prophylactic use of antibiotics before dental work because of mitral valve prolapse or a similar condition, be sure your dentist knows you are pregnant. You must take an antibiotic that is safe for you and your baby. It's best for your dentist and your prenatal care provider to work together on this. (See Prescription Drugs and Medicines, page 104.)

- Vitamin C, which is best used by your body when taken naturally as part of your daily diet, helps tooth and gum tissues to be strong (see page 52).

HEADACHES _____

WHEN

Throughout pregnancy.

1	2	3	4	5	6	7	8	9

WHY

Nasal congestion, fatigue, eyestrain, caffeine withdrawal, anxiety, and tension are all possible causes of headaches during pregnancy (and any other time). In late pregnancy, a sharp, blinding headache that affects your vision may be associated with preeclampsia (see pages 101–2) and should be reported to your care provider.

TRY THIS

- For headaches of the sinus type, press a hot, moist towel over your eyes and forehead. If nasal congestion is part of the problem, a vaporizer may help.

- Rest and relaxation are often the most effective remedies for headaches.

- Pregnancy is not the time to have new glasses or contact lenses fitted, and the lenses that were fine before you became pregnant might cause headache or strain now. Your body's increased volume of circulation during pregnancy can affect your vision, but be reassured that these problems are only temporary.

- Because excessive doses of aspirin may be related to birth defects and problems during pregnancy, some care providers advise against any aspirin use during pregnancy, and suggest a nonaspirin pain reliever such as acetaminophen (Tylenol) instead. There is no conclusive evidence, however, that acetaminophen is really safer than aspirin. After the first trimester, moderate doses of aspirin (up to four per day) are generally considered safe. Don't be afraid to ask for guidance.

- If your headaches persist or are severe, ask your prenatal caregiver what you should do. Don't self-medicate, and don't continue to suffer.

- If the abrupt elimination of caffeine from your diet has left you irritable and with headaches, a more gradual approach to reducing caffeine intake may be appropriate.

HEART POUNDING (PALPITATIONS) _____

WHEN
Mid- to late pregnancy.

1	2	3	4	5	6	7	8	9

WHY

Occasional heart pounding is a normal response your body makes to meeting your baby's needs and the demands of your extra volume of circulation.

TRY THIS

- When you feel your heart pounding, don't panic. Make a conscious effort to let go of tension throughout your body. Sometimes it helps to start at your head and to relax each part of your body in sequence until you reach your toes. Or start at your feet and work up to the top of your head. (See page 74 for suggestions.)

- Breathe easily and comfortably. Take slow, deep breaths. Stay calm.

- If heart pounding is a frequent or continuous problem for you, be sure to tell your prenatal care provider.

HEARTBURN OR INDIGESTION _____

WHEN
Mid- to late pregnancy.

1	2	3	4	5	6	7	8	9

WHY

During pregnancy, your digestive system may work more slowly. Your enlarging uterus crowds your stomach and may cause stomach acids to be pushed upward. Both of these things may lead to heartburn and intestinal gas, or indigestion.

TRY THIS

- Don't crowd your stomach. Eat several small, nourishing meals each day instead of three big ones. Relax and eat slowly. Try to enjoy your meals.

- Avoid spicy, rich, or fried foods or others that tend to cause intestinal gas. You know best which foods disagree with you. Learn from your own mistakes and avoid them.
- Don't lie down directly after eating. When you do lie down, lying on your right side may help the stomach to empty.
- Use good posture. Give your stomach room to work. Try to find positions in which the pressure of your uterus on your stomach is minimized. Sitting in a straight chair, for example, may be better for you than slouching in one that might be very comfortable under different circumstances. You may find that propping yourself up on pillows allows you to sleep more comfortably.
- Wear comfortable clothes that are loose at the waist.
- A very small amount of fatty food (butter or cream, for example) eaten fifteen to thirty minutes before a meal will stimulate digestion and cut down on stomach acid.
- Antacids and bicarbonate of soda or baking soda may cause you to retain fluid and also may bind B vitamins. Avoid them if you can. The very temporary relief such products cause may be followed by heartburn that's even worse than before.
- If you feel you absolutely must take an antacid, try to take it at a time other than mealtime. Avoid products with aspirin, caffeine, or too much sodium (which means nearly everything on the market). Some caregivers suggest Tums, which is a source of supplementary calcium as well as a relatively safe antacid.

HEMORRHOIDS _____

WHEN
Mid- to late pregnancy.

1	2	3	4	5	6	7	8	9

WHY
The increased volume of your circulation causes dilation of veins in your rectum and vagina. There is added pressure from your growing uterus.

TRY THIS
- Try not to become constipated, because constipation will make hemorrhoids more painful. Make an effort not to strain during a bowel movement.
- Use the pelvic floor (Kegel) exercises to strengthen the muscles around your vagina and anus. Tighten this part of your body, hold it for a few seconds, and then relax slowly. Do this at least forty times a day. Try to work up to one hundred times or more. (See pages 68–9.)
- An ice pack (ice cubes tied into a clean handkerchief) may help ease the pain. This works for varicose veins of the vagina as well as for rectal hemorrhoids.
- Cold witch hazel may be soothing. Soak a clean cloth or gauze square and hold it on your hemorrhoids for twenty minutes while you rest, lying down on your left side with your hips on a pillow. Use another pillow to support your arm and hand holding the compress.
- Ask your prenatal care provider if medication such as Preparation H would be appropriate for you at this time in your pregnancy.

LEG CRAMPS

WHEN

Mid- to late pregnancy.

1	2	3	4	5	6	7	8	9

WHY

Calcium, which affects muscle contractions, is less easily absorbed during pregnancy. Pressure from your growing uterus slows circulation in the legs, and this may lead to cramps. Leg cramps often occur when you are in bed.

TRY THIS

- Watch your diet. Be sure to eat foods that are rich in calcium.

- If you take a calcium supplement, it's best to eat foods that contain calcium at the same time. This mineral is best utilized by your body when it is in the presence of other nutrients found around it naturally.

- To ease a cramp in your calf, push away from your body with your heel. At the same time, pull your toes toward your shoulder. This helps stretch the muscle out of its cramp. If you have someone to help you, you can achieve the same effect by having that person press down on your knee with one hand while pushing up against the sole of your foot with the other hand.

- Gentle massage or a hot water bottle on the cramp may help. Try a warm tub bath. (If your cramp is especially severe, you may need someone to help you get in and out of the tub.)

- Avoid lying on your back. The weight of your body and the pressure of your enlarged uterus on major blood vessels will slow down circulation in your legs and increase the likelihood of cramps. Lie on your left side instead.

MORNING SICKNESS (SEE NAUSEA AND VOMITING)

NAUSEA AND VOMITING

WHEN

First three months.

1	2	3	4	5	6	7	8	9

WHY

Your body may be reacting to the hormones of pregnancy. Too little Vitamin B_6 or too little glycogen, the natural sugar stored in your liver, can cause nausea. Emotions are another possible cause of nausea during pregnancy.

TRY THIS

- Nausea is especially bothersome on an empty stomach, so you might try a high-protein snack such as lean meat or cheese before going to bed. (Protein takes longer to digest.)

- If you are troubled by nausea in the morning (morning sickness), nibble on some crackers, toast, or dry cereal about 20 to 30 minutes before you get out of bed.

- Eat small but frequent meals during the day instead of three large ones. Eat slowly, chew your food completely, and try to stay relaxed. Avoid fried, spicy, or rich foods or any food that seems to give you indigestion.

- Drink your fruit juice after breakfast instead of at the beginning. Some women find it best not to drink liquids with their food, but to take fluids between meals instead. Find out what works for you and do it.

- Extra Vitamin B_6 may be helpful.

- If your vomiting is persistent and so severe that you find you can't keep food or fluids down on a continuous basis, consult your prenatal caregiver. Get help before you become seriously dehydrated.

NOSEBLEEDS

WHEN

Throughout pregnancy.

1	2	3	4	5	6	7	8	9

WHY

Membranes become overloaded during pregnancy from the increased volume of circulation. In some women, this causes nosebleeds.

TRY THIS

- Be sure you are getting enough vitamin C in your diet (see page 52). Vitamin C promotes strong tissues.

- To stop a nosebleed, pinch your nostrils together for several minutes. When the bleeding stops, lie down and apply cold compresses to your nose. This may prevent an immediate recurrence.

- If suffering from nasal congestion, be careful to blow your nose gently rather than with vigor.

- A higher level of humidity will help decrease the risk of nosebleeds. If the air in your home tends to be very dry, try a humidifier.

- Try a thin coating of Vaseline in each nostril, especially at bedtime.

PELVIC PAIN OR DISCOMFORT

WHEN

Mid- to late pregnancy.

1	2	3	4	5	6	7	8	9

WHY

During pregnancy, your pelvic joints relax to increase the size and flexibility of space available for the birth canal. This may cause pressure on the sciatic nerve, with pain in the pelvic area and down the thigh into the leg. Another source of discomfort may be the pressure of your growing uterus on the ligaments that support it. This may cause sharp, shooting pains on either side of your abdomen.

TRY THIS

- Warmth may help you relax and bring some relief. Try a hot water bottle or a warm tub bath.

- Some women find massage helpful.

- Try the wheelbarrow exercise. You'll need your partner's help for this one. (See page 73 for detailed directions.)

- A change in position may help you. Experiment with different positions to find the one that brings you the most relief. Sit for a while with your feet elevated. Try sleeping on your side, with one leg forward and the other back, as if you were running.

- If you are constipated or have a bladder infection, you also may experience some discomfort in the pelvic region. See pages 22–4 and 61 for suggestions on dealing with discomfort.

- If your pain is so severe or persistent that you can't stand it, consult your prenatal caregiver. Don't self-medicate or continue to suffer.

SALIVATION (EXCESSIVE) _____

WHEN
   Mid- to late pregnancy.

1	2	3	4	5	6	7	8	9

WHY

   During pregnancy, the salivary glands increase production. For a few women, this increase may turn out to be excessive. The reason for this is unclear.

TRY THIS

- Chewing gum may help keep excessive salivation under control.

- Sometimes eating several small meals instead of three large ones during the day will help with this problem.

SHORTNESS OF BREATH _____

WHEN
   Mid- to late pregnancy—in the ninth month, after your baby drops, you may find some relief.

1	2	3	4	5	6	7	8	9

WHY

Your growing uterus takes up part of your breathing space, causing pressure on your diaphragm.

TRY THIS

- Hold your arms up over your head and stretch. This raises your rib cage and temporarily gives you more breathing space.

- Find positions that give you more room to breathe. Sitting up in a straight chair may work. Try sleeping propped up with pillows in a position that makes breathing easier. If you're not comfortable propped up with pillows, try lying on your left side instead. Experiment with different positions until you find one that works for you. (But don't lie flat on your back.)

- Practice very slow, deep breathing while you are relaxed. Try this every day. It will help you use your lung space to its greatest capacity.

- When you become short of breath, you may find you just have to slow down. Don't race up the stairs; walk slowly. Don't exert yourself. Listen to your body.

SKIN (BLOTCHES AND DISCOLORING)

WHEN
Mid- to late pregnancy.

1	2	3	4	5	6	7	8	9

WHY

A high level of pregnancy hormones can trigger extra deposits of pigment, which may appear as darkened blotches on the cheeks, nose, and forehead as well as on the nipples and in a line from the navel to the pubic bone. These skin changes may be associated with an inadequate supply of folic acid as well as the increase in pregnancy hormones.

TRY THIS

- Exposure to the sun makes the condition more intense. Avoid sunburn.

- Make sure that your diet contains sufficient sources of folic acid (see page 62). The daily requirement for folic acid doubles during pregnancy.

- If dark blotches on your face make you self-conscious about your appearance, try the type of cream makeup designed to minimize birthmarks.

- Be reassured that the hormone that causes these discolorations will decrease after your baby is born. The spots will disappear of their own accord.

STRETCH MARKS

WHEN
Mid- to late pregnancy.

1	2	3	4	5	6	7	8	9

WHY

About 90 percent of pregnant women experience stretch marks to some degree. Stretch marks are a type of scar tissue that forms when the skin's normal elasticity is not sufficient to accommodate the stretching required during pregnancy. Stretch marks occur most frequently on the abdomen, but some women also get them on the breasts, buttocks, or thighs.

TRY THIS

• Be sure that your diet contains adequate sources of the nutrients needed for healthy skin—primarily vitamin C and vitamin E (see pages 52–3). Sufficient protein is essential, too.

• Understand that stretch marks are caused from within, and external treatments can't remove or prevent them. Money spent on expensive or exotic skin creams may make you feel like you're doing something, but it won't make the stretch marks disappear.

• Even though keeping your skin soft and supple won't prevent stretch marks, it might help minimize them and it may help you feel better about yourself. Some women find that cocoa butter helps keep the skin soft. A gentle massage with oil or cream—on your own or with the help of your mate—may be pleasurable and relaxing as well as an aid to soft, smooth skin.

• Although stretch marks may not disappear after delivery, those that remain usually fade into a light silver color.

SWELLING (FEET, LEGS, AND HANDS) _____

WHEN

Mid- to late pregnancy.

| 1 | 2 | 3 | 4 | 5 | 6 | 7 | 8 | 9 |

WHY

Fluid retention that causes swelling (edema) is a natural condition of pregnancy. The growing uterus puts pressure on the blood vessels that carry fluid from the feet and ankles. Tight clothing, especially around the ankles, legs, and lower body, can increase fluid retention and swelling by slowing down circulation. Too little protein in the diet may cause the body to retain fluid.

TRY THIS

• Don't remain on your feet for long periods of time. To help reduce swelling, sit with your legs and feet raised. If you can't sit with your feet up as often as you would like, walking around will stimulate circulation. Avoid standing still in one place if you can. Some form of mild to moderate physical activity will help to pump out excess fluid.

• When you sit, try to elevate your feet and legs. Don't sit with your feet on the floor for extended periods. Don't cross your legs when you sit, because this can further interfere with your already sluggish circulation.

- Wear loose, comfortable clothing. Be sure to avoid tight pants, snug waistbands, garters, knee or ankle socks with tight bands, or anything else that might constrict your circulation.

- A wedge-shaped pillow under the mattress at the foot of your bed will enable you to rest with your feet elevated. Lying on your left side may help, too.

- Be sure to keep your daily diet rich in protein.

- Although fluid retention during pregnancy was at one time thought to be related to excess salt intake, that view is no longer considered correct. Salt restriction during pregnancy does not cure edema and actually may cause harm (see pages 55 and 63). You may salt your food to taste, in moderation.

- You can't prevent or reduce edema by avoiding fluids. In fact, the opposite is true. Drinking clear fluids (water) will help your kidneys work well and pull the extra fluid out of your system (see page 61).

- Some swelling of the feet, ankles, and legs is to be expected and is probably not cause for concern unless the various measures suggested above are ineffective. Let your prenatal care provider know immediately, however, if your hands or face swell up. This may be a warning sign that your kidneys are not functioning as efficiently as they should be.

TIREDNESS

WHEN

Early and late pregnancy.

1	2	3	4	5	6	7	8	9

WHY

Fatigue is a natural effect of the hormones of pregnancy. Carrying and caring for your developing baby requires extra energy. Tiredness also may result from anemia, which is not uncommon during pregnancy.

TRY THIS
- Early to bed, late to rise, with rest periods during the day as well.

- Balance your rest with daily exercise. (Brisk walking is excellent.) Exercise stimulates circulation and brings oxygen and nutrition to your entire body.

- Have your prenatal care provider check you for anemia. If anemia is a problem for you, changes in your diet and/or supplementary iron may be suggested.

- Vary your position and your activities if you can. For example, if your work requires you to be on your feet for long periods, try to schedule short rests during which you can sit down with your feet up. If, on the other hand, you must spend a lot of time sitting, try to get up and walk around every hour or so.

- Try to do whatever you must do efficiently, but don't be afraid to share chores and burdens with family members or friends. Admit (at least to yourself) that you cannot and need not be supermom at all times.

VAGINAL DISCHARGE

WHEN
Throughout pregnancy.

1	2	3	4	5	6	7	8	9

WHY
Increased blood supply and hormones cause your vagina to increase its normal secretions. The normally acidic atmosphere of the vagina changes, too, creating a more fertile setting for the common vaginal infection monilia (yeast infection).

TRY THIS
- Wear skirts rather than slacks or jeans, which are tight in the crotch. Air circulation will help.

- Cotton briefs or at least those with a cotton crotch are better than underpants made of synthetic fabrics.

- Frequent baths (warm, not too hot) will keep you feeling clean. A minipad or panty shield will add to your comfort and make you feel more secure.

- Do not douche during pregnancy, because it is possible at this time to introduce air into your circulatory system or, in the later months, to break your bag of waters (see page 88). If a douche is medically necessary for you at any time during your pregnancy, your prenatal care provider will explain exactly how the procedure should be done to minimize the risks.

- If your discharge burns, itches, smells bad, or causes your genitals to become swollen or inflamed, call your prenatal caregiver. You probably have a yeast infection, but it's important to find out for sure so that the correct treatment can be prescribed.

- If you do have a yeast infection, cutting out sugar and wheat products may help. Plain natural yogurt, both as part of your diet and applied vaginally, may help reduce itching. Medication for yeast infections, once available only by prescription, can now be purchased over the counter. It's probably best to consult your prenatal caregiver before using such a remedy.

- Be alert to the signs of preterm labor (see page 122). Call your prenatal care provider without delay to report an increase or change in vaginal discharge, especially if the discharge is clear and watery or tinged with blood.

VARICOSE VEINS

WHEN
Mid- to late pregnancy.

1	2	3	4	5	6	7	8	9

WHY
Veins in your legs can become overloaded as a result of the slowed circulation caused by the greater volume of blood and the pressure of your growing uterus.

TRY THIS

- Avoid standing for long periods. If you must stand, try to move about.
- Avoid remaining in any position that might restrict the circulation in your legs. For example, don't sit with your thighs pressed against the edge of a chair and don't cross your legs when you sit.
- Rest several times a day with your feet up and your legs raised at a mild angle to your body.
- Leg and foot exercises will help your blood to circulate better (see pages 70–1).
- Elastic stockings may help. You should put them on before you get out of bed in the morning, while your legs are still relatively free of the extra blood that overloads them when you stand.

NUTRITION FOR YOU AND YOUR BABY _____

What you eat or don't eat during pregnancy affects your health and comfort and really does make a difference to your developing baby. Although some people mistakenly believe an unborn child can draw all needed nourishment from the mother's body even if she eats poorly, it simply isn't so. If your diet lacks essential nutrients, your baby will suffer the effects along with you.

At one time it was thought that the placenta served as a barrier to protect the fetus from harmful substances taken by the mother, but this isn't so, either. Virtually everything a pregnant woman eats or drinks will reach her baby in some way.

The effects of poor nutrition are passed from one generation to the next. What your mother ate before you were born, what you ate throughout your growing years, as well as your present diet all influence your unborn child.

If for any reason your diet was inadequate in the past, you can't go back and do things over again. But you can start now, if you haven't already done so, to plan your meals carefully so that you and your baby will be well nourished. The Food Guide Pyramid can help you.

The Food Guide Pyramid depicts a research-based plan for healthful eating that was developed by expert nutritionists at the U.S. Department of Agriculture (USDA) and the Department of Health and Human Services (HHS). The Pyramid provides basic nutritional information in a format designed to make it easy for anyone—pregnant or not—to make appropriate and healthful food choices on a daily basis. Here's how it works.

Each block of the Pyramid represents a food group, and you should choose foods from each group every day. Each of the food groups provides some of the nutrients you need, but not all of them. That's why it's important to balance your choices over the course of a day so you don't omit anything you and your baby need.

FOOD GUIDE PYRAMID ... BLOCK BY BLOCK __

The material that follows explains the Food Guide Pyramid, block by block and level by level, to make it easy for you to use. For each food group, you will find the number of servings you need each day during pregnancy along with examples of what counts as a serving. Note that these examples are for counting purposes and are not necessarily the amount of a food you would serve at a meal. A spaghetti dinner, for example, might count as two or even three servings of pasta, depending on how generous the portion.

You don't need to spend time weighing or measuring the servings exactly. Use common sense. For mixed dishes, make your best guess. A macaroni and cheese casserole with tuna, for example, might count as one serving each in the bread group (macaroni), the meat group (tuna), and the milk group (cheese). If it's actually a little more pasta and a little less meat, don't worry about it. Over the course of a day or two, things will probably even out.

These guidelines are intended to help you achieve a balanced diet. As you make your choices within each food group, try to remember which foods are especially rich in essential nutrients, and include them often (the information on pages 48–56 will help). If you eat a variety of carefully chosen foods from the different food groups, your diet is likely to provide the nutrients you need.

Food Guide Pyramid

A Guide to Daily Food Choices

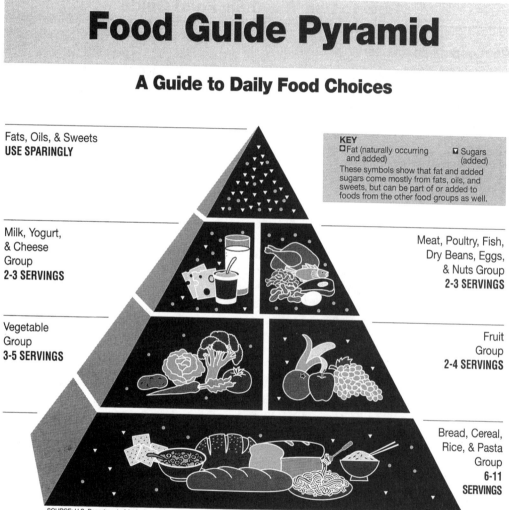

Fats, Oils, & Sweets
USE SPARINGLY

KEY
☐ Fat (naturally occurring and added) ☑ Sugars (added)
These symbols show that fat and added sugars come mostly from fats, oils, and sweets, but can be part of or added to foods from the other food groups as well.

Milk, Yogurt, & Cheese Group
2-3 SERVINGS

Meat, Poultry, Fish, Dry Beans, Eggs, & Nuts Group
2-3 SERVINGS

Vegetable Group
3-5 SERVINGS

Fruit Group
2-4 SERVINGS

Bread, Cereal, Rice, & Pasta Group
6-11 SERVINGS

SOURCE: U.S. Department of Agriculture/U.S. Department of Health and Human Services

BREAD GROUP

The base of the Pyramid, the foundation of a healthy diet, contains breads, cereals, rice, and pasta. These are all foods from grains. For the general population, the range of servings in this group is six to eleven per day. During pregnancy, your daily goal should be at least nine servings.

Bread, Cereal,
Rice, and Pasta
Group
6—11
Servings

WHAT COUNTS AS ONE SERVING?

1 slice bread
½ cup cooked pasta
½ cup cooked cereal
½ cup cooked rice
1 ounce ready-to-eat cereal

To maximize the nutrients and natural fiber you get from your servings, concentrate on using whole grains as much as you can. Whole wheat bread, for example, is more nutritious than white bread. Brown or wild rice is preferable to refined white rice. You can increase the nutrient density of foods you prepare yourself by using whole grain flour instead of highly processed white flour or by adding wheat germ to everything from baked goods to cereals, meatloaf, and casseroles.

If you are wondering how you will ever manage to get down nine servings a day of the bread group, take a look again at what counts as a serving. If you eat some crackers before you get out of bed to ease a queasy stomach, that's already one serving. A small dish of cereal and a piece of toast for breakfast adds two more. A lunchtime sandwich counts as two servings from the bread group (along with a serving or more from whatever group covers the filling). A cup of pasta along with a roll or slice of bread at the evening meal adds three more servings. A few more crackers, a muffin, or another piece of toast as a snack would give you the nine.

VEGETABLE GROUP

The Food Guide Pyramid suggests a general range of three to five servings per day from the vegetable group. During pregnancy, you should try for at least four servings daily. Vary your vegetable selections, because different types of vegetables provide different nutrients. You need leafy green vegetables (spinach, broccoli, kale, collard greens, romaine lettuce, chicory), deep yellow vegetables (carrots, yams, sweet potatoes, acorn squash), and starchy vegetables (potatoes, corn, peas, lima beans), along with miscellaneous others (tomatoes, onions, green or yellow beans, zucchini). You don't need every type of vegetable every day, but don't omit any category for longer than a day or two.

Legumes (chickpeas and kidney, pinto, or navy beans) can be used as a protein source as well as a source of vitamins and minerals. You can count legumes as vegetables or substitute them for meat in the meat group.

WHAT COUNTS AS ONE SERVING?

½ cup cooked vegetables
½ cup chopped raw vegetables
1 cup leafy raw vegetables

Vegetable
Group
3–5 Servings

Fresh vegetables eaten raw or minimally cooked (steamed briefly or microwaved) are your best source of nutrients and fiber. Frozen vegetables without sauces or additives are also excellent choices and are best if you can't get high-quality fresh produce. Canned or dehydrated vegetables may have added sugar and salt and are likely to have lost some nutrients in processing. Don't cancel out the benefits of vegetables by cooking them in oil or loading them up with butter or margarine. Remember to count any added cooking oils or toppings such as mayonnaise, salad dressing, butter, or margarine in your allotment at the top of the Pyramid to be "used sparingly."

FRUIT GROUP

Fruits and fruit juices are sources of key nutrients such as vitamin C, vitamin A, and potassium. The Food Guide Pyramid suggests a range of two to four servings per day. During pregnancy you should choose at least three times from the fruit group every day.

WHAT COUNTS AS ONE SERVING?

1 medium-size apple, pear, or orange
½ grapefruit
1 melon wedge
1 banana
½ cup chopped, cooked, or canned fruit
¾ cup (6 ounces) pure fruit juice
¼ cup dried fruit, such as raisins or prunes

Fruit
Group
2–4 Servings

Fruit drinks, punches, or ades don't count as a serving of fruit because they are mostly sugar.

If you need more fiber, remember that whole fruits (fresh or dried) provide more fiber than fruit juices do. Avoid canned fruits packed in heavy syrup, unless you have lots of leftover sugar allotment to spare. Remember that fruit punches and ades aren't fruit; they're fruit-flavored sugar water. Stick with unsweetened, natural fruit juices.

MILK GROUP

During pregnancy, the milk group in the Food Guide Pyramid is especially important. Milk products are the best source of calcium as well as a source of protein, vitamins, and other nutrients.

WHAT COUNTS AS ONE SERVING?

Milk, Yogurt, and Cheese Group
2–3 Servings

    1 cup milk (whole or skim)
    1 cup yogurt
    1½ ounces natural cheese
    2 ounces processed cheese

    1 cup cottage cheese counts as ½ serving of milk because it has less calcium than milk.

In making food choices from the milk group, try to limit your fat intake while maximizing calcium and protein. Choose skim milk and lowfat or nonfat yogurt more often than whole milk. Ice cream counts in the milk group, but it also counts at the tip of the Pyramid in the fat group. Ice milk or frozen yogurt may be a better choice.

MEAT GROUP

The Food Guide Pyramid suggests two to three servings per day from the group, including meat, poultry, fish, dried beans, eggs, and nuts. During pregnancy you should have at least two daily servings, perhaps three. If you have just two servings, the amounts involved should be toward the larger end of the range of what counts as a serving.

WHAT COUNTS AS ONE SERVING?

Meat, Poultry, Fish, Dried Beans, Eggs, and Nuts Group
2–3 Servings

    2–3 ounces cooked lean meat
    2–3 ounces cooked poultry
    2–3 ounces cooked fish

    Count 1 egg, ½ cup cooked dried beans, or 2 tablespoons peanut butter as 1 ounce lean meat (about ⅓ serving).

    As a rule of thumb, a 4-ounce piece of meat is roughly the size of a deck of cards, so 2–3 ounces would be slightly smaller than that.

Your meat choices should be lean and prepared without additional fat. Broil, roast, poach, or boil rather than fry. Trim any visible fat before cooking. Poultry without skin is preferable. Fish (broiled, steamed, poached) is an excellent lowfat choice.

Canned fish (such as tuna) packed in oil may be rinsed to reduce fat content. Similar fish packed in spring water would be better. Even if you really enjoy rare or raw meat and fish, pregnancy is not a time to take any such risks with food safety. It's best to cook your hamburgers thoroughly and to stay away from sushi restaurants until after your baby is born.

FATS, OILS, AND SWEETS

Throughout the Food Guide Pyramid, you will find little symbols for fats (naturally occurring and added) and sugars (added). These symbols appear occasionally in each of the food groups, showing that fats and sugars can occur naturally or be added to each of the food groups. The highest concentration, however, is at the tip of the Pyramid. This is where you keep track of the fats, oils, and sugars that you add to what you eat. This is where you can and should exercise some control.

You should limit the calories you get from fat to 25 to 30 percent of your daily total. If you choose wisely within the various groups in the Food Guide Pyramid, you will be able to keep your daily fat intake within the recommended range. If, for example, your fat intake tends to be higher than it should be, use lowfat or nonfat yogurt and buy skim milk instead of whole milk. Choose fish or poultry in preference to red meat. Don't load up your whole wheat bread with butter, margarine, or mayonnaise. Garnish your steamed or microwaved vegetables with lemon instead of butter or margarine. Use added fats and oils (the group at the Pyramid's tip) sparingly, if at all.

Fats, Oils, and Sweets
Use Sparingly

Key
◻ Fat (naturally occurring and added)
◪ Sugars (added)
These symbols show that fat and added sugars come mostly from fats, oils, and sweets, but can be part of or added to foods from the other food groups as well.

What does the directive "use sparingly" mean with respect to added sugars? If your suggested daily caloric intake is about two thousand calories, you should try to limit added sugars from all sources to ten teaspoons or less. As the caloric requirement increases, you may add a teaspoon for each hundred-calorie increase. Note that these guidelines are averages over time, not precise prescriptions for any given day. If you can cut your sugar intake even further, so much the better. If a piece of chocolate cake or a fast-food shake should fill up the pyramid's tip with a week's worth of extras in a weekend, try to get your food choices back into balance as soon as you can.

OLESTRA ALERT

If you are tempted to reduce your calorie count and fat intake by consuming snacks formulated with the new fat substitute olestra, there is just one word of advice: Don't! Despite recent FDA approval of olestra in savory snacks such as potato chips and crackers, there are serious reasons to avoid such items. As olestra passes through the body, it steals away essential nutrients such as the fat-soluble vitamins A, D, E, and K, and beta carotene. In addition to its negative nutritional impact, olestra may produce unpleasant and potentially harmful side effects such as diarrhea, cramping, and anal leakage. You don't need olestra at any time, and certainly not when you're pregnant.

PERSONAL DIET DIAGNOSIS _____

Follow these steps to analyze the adequacy of your own diet:

1. In the space below, keep a list of everything you eat and drink during a day. Do what you normally would do during this time; don't change your eating habits just because you're writing things down. Remember that what you want here is an accurate picture of your food choice patterns.

FOOD LIST	COMMENTS (See Step 3)

2. At the end of the day, look at your list and transfer each item to its correct block in the blank Food Guide Pyramid below. See how your food choices fit. Do you have enough entries in each of the key blocks? Do you have too many in the Pyramid's point?

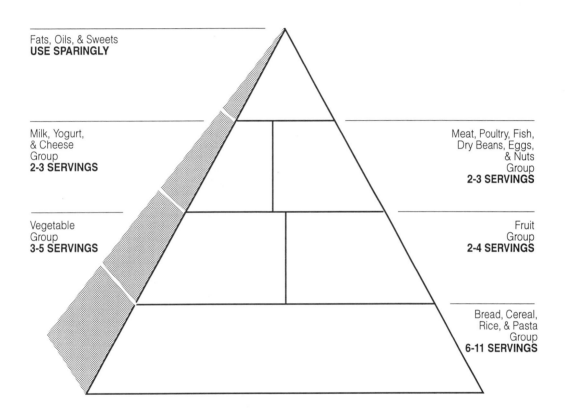

Fats, Oils, & Sweets
USE SPARINGLY

Milk, Yogurt,
& Cheese
Group
2-3 SERVINGS

Meat, Poultry, Fish,
Dry Beans, Eggs,
& Nuts
Group
2-3 SERVINGS

Vegetable
Group
3-5 SERVINGS

Fruit
Group
2-4 SERVINGS

Bread, Cereal,
Rice, & Pasta
Group
6-11 SERVINGS

3. Check your food choices again. Did you get enough protein? Calcium? Iron? Vitamin C? Folic acid? Other B vitamins? Refer to the text (see pages 48–59) that discusses each of these nutrients if you wish. On your original list, note in the comments section any changes you would make if you had it to do over again.

DAILY DIET TALLY

Throughout pregnancy, you may use the Personal Diet Diagnosis (pages 44–5) whenever you wish, to study your food choices carefully and to help you make whatever dietary changes you might need at that point for your optimum health and for that of your developing baby. Most people, however, do not need to do an in-depth analysis of their diet on a continuous or long-term basis. Once you understand how to use the Food Guide Pyramid, a simple tally of the servings you eat in each of the food groups each day should be sufficient.

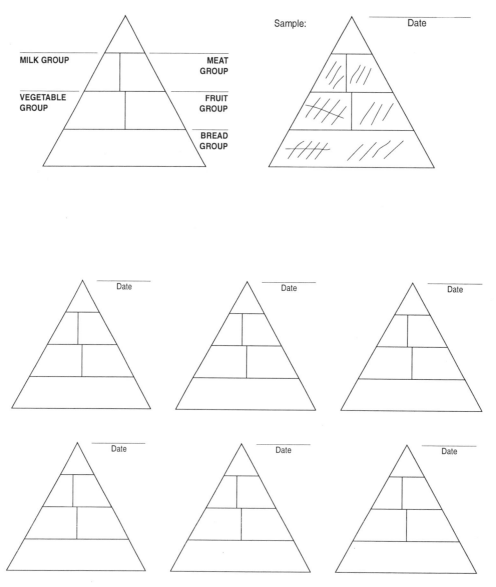

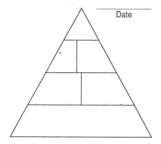 Date _____

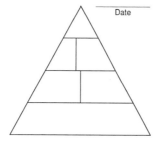 Date _____

Date _____

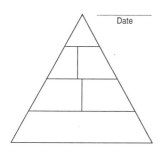 Date _____

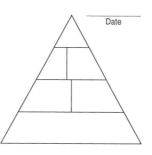 Date _____

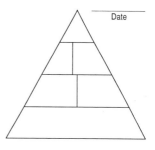 Date _____

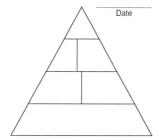 Date _____

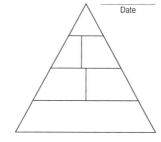 Date _____

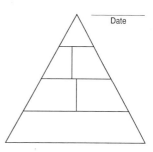 Date _____

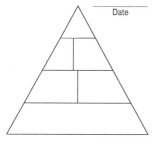 Date _____

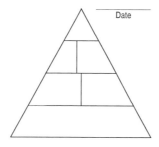 Date _____

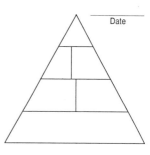 Date _____

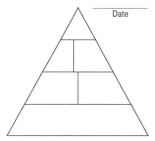 Date _____

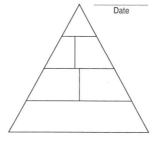 Date _____

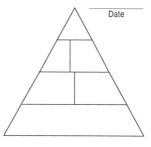 Date _____

NUTRIENTS YOU AND YOUR BABY NEED _____

The Food Guide Pyramid is your guide to healthful food choices during pregnancy or any other time. Although most people can successfully follow the Pyramid without an in-depth understanding of each of the nutrients involved, you may find it helpful to learn more about each of the components of good nutrition.

The material that follows describes the nutrients—carbohydrates, proteins, fats, vitamins, and minerals—you need, explains the role each plays in pregnancy, and identifies appropriate food sources. The material here will help you understand the rationale behind the Food Guide Pyramid's food groups. When you read about calcium, for example, you will see why you are advised to choose at least three servings from the milk group each day. When you read about the B vitamins and various minerals, you will understand the reason you are advised to make sure many of your bread, cereal, and pasta choices involve whole grains rather than highly refined products.

To maximize your benefits from following the Food Guide Pyramid, you must do more than choose the suggested number of servings from each food group. You must also make certain that your choices within each group are the best they can be for your circumstances. The specific information about each nutrient you need will help you do that.

CARBOHYDRATES _____

Carbohydrates, an essential part of the diet, are perhaps the most misunderstood of the necessary nutrients. More than half of your daily caloric intake should come from carbohydrates, the fuel that gives your body energy. There are two categories of carbohydrates: starches and sugars. These groups are by no means equal or interchangeable, however, in terms of meeting your nutritional needs.

Complex carbohydrates, or starches, are the basic foundation of a healthful diet. Complex carbohydrates provide a steady source of energy for you and your developing baby. You will find complex carbohydrates in whole grains—the bread, cereal, rice, and pasta group depicted at the base of the Food Guide Pyramid—and in vegetables and fruits, the food groups next to the base. Foods containing complex carbohydrates also tend to be rich sources of other key nutrients, especially the B vitamins and vitamin C.

Simple carbohydrates, or sugars, can be a source of quick energy, but the boost they provide tends to be short-lived. Worst of all from a nutritional standpoint are refined sugars, which provide sweetness, empty calories, and nothing for your baby to grow on. It's better, if you can, to satisfy your craving for sweet food with a piece of fresh fruit rather than a candy bar, dessert, or soft drink made with refined sugar. Along with the energy from the fruit's natural sugars, you get needed vitamins and minerals as well as dietary fiber.

As you plan what you will eat throughout your pregnancy, carbohydrates should play a major role. For each serving of a food rich in carbohydrates, however, remember that what you want is complex carbohydrates that are dense in nutrients, not simple carbohydrates that are sweet but nutritionally empty.

PROTEIN

Proteins are complex chemicals that have two important functions. One function is to serve as the building materials of body tissue. From your hair to your toenails, most of your body—your bones, blood, muscles, and other tissues—is made up primarily of proteins. The second function is to act as enzymes that regulate the chemical reactions that keep a body growing and functioning.

When you understand the two roles proteins play, it's easy to see how important this nutrient would be for an unborn child. A developing fetus is building new tissue and experiencing chemical reactions at a very rapid rate. Proteins are vital to these processes.

Too little protein in a pregnant woman's diet can harm both the quality and quantity of her baby's growth. Proteins are essential for the production of brain cells, and a child's future mental capacity may be influenced by protein in the mother's diet. An adequate prenatal supply of protein is directly related to building strong bones and teeth.

Proteins are made up of substances called amino acids. More than twenty different amino acids have been identified. Your body's cells can manufacture all but eight of these. These eight, called essential amino acids, must be supplied by your food. Complete proteins are those that contain adequate supplies of these eight essential amino acids. Incomplete proteins are those that lack or have too little of one or more essential amino acids.

If you eat an incomplete protein at the same time as a complete one, your body can combine amino acids to form additional complete proteins. Macaroni and cheese or cereal and milk are examples of how you could combine an incomplete protein with a complete one. Certain combinations of two or more incomplete proteins also will work to form complete proteins, but these combinations are useful only when one food source supplies the amino acids missing in the other. Baked beans and cornbread or peanut butter on whole wheat bread are examples of combinations of incomplete proteins that complement each other to form complete proteins.

What should be your daily protein intake during pregnancy? A daily protein intake of approximately 70 to 80 grams of protein for pregnant women has been recommended by the Food and Nutrition Board of the National Academy of Sciences. This represents an increase of 30 grams per day over the amount recommended for the nonpregnant woman. Some nutritionists, however, consider these figures to be too low and recommend 90 to 100 grams of protein per day, especially during the last half of pregnancy. The increase in need is gradual. As the baby increases in size, the protein requirement increases.

If you have questions about what your protein intake should be, ask your prenatal care provider for additional guidance. The groups in the Food Guide Pyramid are designed to ensure enough protein in a person's daily diet. Because protein needs are increased during pregnancy, it is important to choose your protein-rich foods carefully. You should aim for the higher number of servings in the suggested range of the protein-intensive blocks of the pyramid. (These are the milk, yogurt, and cheese group and the meat, poultry, fish, dried beans, eggs, and nuts group. Careful choices in the bread, cereal, rice, and pasta group also can enhance your protein intake.)

FATS

Fat plays an important role in body tissues. Fats provide energy and will aid both you and your developing baby in absorbing calcium and the fat-soluble vitamins (A, D, E, and K). Fats are found in animal protein foods such as milk, meat, and egg yolks. Other important sources in the diet are grains, nuts, seeds, and the oils made from them.

A fat-free diet would be unhealthful and impossible to achieve. Among the nutrients supplied by fats in your diet is linoleic acid, an essential fatty acid that your body can't manufacture on its own. Most people, however, consume far more fat than they need. In this country, unhealthful food consumption patterns in which 40 percent or more of the calories come from fats are not uncommon.

Food fats are mixtures of three types of fatty acids—polyunsaturated, monounsaturated, and saturated. Diets that are excessively high in fats, especially saturated fats, are associated with obesity, heart disease, and various forms of cancer. The largest amounts of saturated fats are found in foods from animal sources (meat and dairy) and certain tropical vegetable oils, such as palm oil or coconut oil.

It is recommended that no more than 30 percent of the calories in a person's daily food intake be derived from fat. Some nutritionists suggest reducing that amount to 25 percent. Only a third of the total fat intake should be from saturated fats. During pregnancy, as at other times, it would be wise to limit the calories you get from fat to 25 to 30 percent of your daily total.

If you choose wisely within the various groups in the Food Guide Pyramid, you will be able to keep your daily fat intake within the recommended range. If, for example, your fat intake tends to be higher than it should be, use lowfat or nonfat yogurt and use skim milk instead of whole milk. Choose fish or poultry in preference to red meat. Don't load up your whole wheat bread with butter, margarine, or mayonnaise. Top your salads and vegetables with lemon juice instead of oily dressings and butter or margarine. Use added fats and oils (the group at the Pyramid's tip) sparingly, if at all.

VITAMIN A

Vitamin A, which is necessary for the growth and repair of cell membranes, plays an important role in fetal development and in your own well-being. Vitamin A helps to maintain the health and the soft, moist condition of cells in the outer layers of skin and in the lining of the stomach, intestines, respiratory system, and liver. Vitamin A is related to the health of the eyes and the prevention of "night blindness."

The best dietary sources of vitamin A are fish liver oil, beef and chicken liver, orange or yellow vegetables, orange or yellow fruits, and leafy green vegetables. Other food sources of vitamin A include egg yolks, fortified milk, butter or margarine, and some cheeses.

Vitamin A is fragile and sensitive to air. Prolonged exposure to air or heat from cooking can destroy much of the vitamin before it reaches the table and you. To preserve as much vitamin A as possible during food preparation, cook vegetables briefly if at all, use covered containers, and serve promptly.

Vitamin A is a fat-soluble vitamin, which means that the body requires the presence of dietary fats in order to use this vitamin. You should, however, avoid taking mineral oil, because mineral oil is not absorbed by the body and can bind vitamin A and the other fat-soluble vitamins (D, E, and K) and carry them off so they can't be used as they pass through your digestive system.

Beta-carotene, the pigment that gives vegetables such as carrots, sweet potatoes, and squash their color, is a naturally occurring dietary chemical the body can convert to usable vitamin A. It is beta-carotene that makes the yellow vegetables and fruits such a rich and safe food source of vitamin A.

Because an excess of vitamin A can be stored in body tissues and may cause harm, you should not self-prescribe supplements of this individual vitamin. Excessive dosages of vitamin A have been linked to birth defects. If you take a prescribed prenatal vitamin supplement, it will be formulated to keep the vitamin A intake within appropriate limits. Food sources of vitamin A, unless consumed in extraordinary excess, will not cause an overdose. If you follow the Food Guide Pyramid and obtain your vitamin A (or beta-carotene) from food sources such as yellow vegetables in the recommended amounts, you will be able to get the amount of this nutrient you need safely.

B VITAMINS _____

The B complex vitamins include thiamine (B_1), riboflavin (B_2), niacin, vitamin B_6, folacin (folic acid), biotin, vitamin B_{12}, and pantothenic acid. An adequate supply during pregnancy is necessary for proper cell division and fetal growth. B vitamins aid the body in responding to stress. This can be especially important to you during pregnancy. These vitamins will assist you in digesting carbohydrates and protein.

Folacin, which is needed for making DNA and RNA, is a vital nutrient, especially during pregnancy. A woman's need for the B vitamin folic acid doubles during pregnancy (see page 62). A deficiency of folic acid has been linked to a higher than normal risk of having a baby with neural tube defects.

Women whose diets are high in protein but low in complex carbohdyrates and vitamin B_6 may experience more nausea of pregnancy (morning sickness) than those whose intake of this vitamin is sufficient (see page 29). Severe prenatal deficiencies of vitamin B_6 have been associated with blood disorders and mental retardation. Although the causes of preeclampsia (see pages 101–2) have not been identified with certainty, malnourished women may be at a higher risk for this condition. The B vitamins play an important role in the body's ability to utilize key nutrients.

The B vitamins are water soluble, and excesses are passed out with urine rather than being stored in the body. For this reason, daily intake is necessary. Another important fact to remember about the B vitamins is that they work together as a team, so an individual one should not be omitted or ingested in significantly larger doses than the others.

Dietary sources of the B vitamins include whole, unrefined grains (cracked and whole wheat, brown rice, rye, wheat germ), liver and other organ meats, leafy vegetables, milk, and eggs. The B vitamins are quite fragile and are easily destroyed by refining processes and cooking. Because of this, it may be difficult to be certain you are getting enough in your diet even if you choose foods wisely and try to prepare them carefully. Many care providers suggest a prenatal vitamin supplement as a safeguard.

VITAMIN C

Vitamin C in sufficient supply is needed for strong cell walls and blood vessels. Vitamin C helps the body utilize iron, folic acid, and vitamin A. Tender gums and nosebleeds, both common discomforts of pregnancy, often can be controlled by an increased intake of vitamin C. The need for vitamin C is further increased by stress, disease, or smoking.

You will find vitamin C in citrus fruits (grapefruit, oranges, lemons, limes, tangerines), melons (cantaloupe, watermelon), strawberries, tomatoes, potatoes, broccoli, bell peppers, cabbage, and kale. Because the body does not store vitamin C, you need a fresh supply of this vitamin every day.

Vitamin C is easily destroyed by heat and contact with the air. It dissolves in liquid. You will need, therefore, to be careful in preparing vegetables containing vitamin C. Cook them minimally, using as little water as possible. Use a covered container and serve immediately after preparation.

During pregnancy, you should confine your intake of supplementary vitamin C to what is recommended by your care provider even if you comfortably take very large doses at other times. Remember that the fetus is very small, and what is a safe dose for an adult could be very much more than an unborn child can handle. The baby whose system must work hard to deal with overdoses of vitamin C before birth may have trouble using vitamin C effectively later.

VITAMIN D

Vitamin D is required to regulate the body's absorption of calcium. Perhaps the best natural source of vitamin D is sunlight, although it may not be practical to rely on the sun for what you need. If you spend time in the sunlight, vitamin D can be absorbed through your skin. Most milk sold commercially is fortified with vitamin D, and this is probably the best way to get what you need in your daily diet. In addition to fortified milk, food sources of vitamin D include egg yolks, liver, fortified butter or margarine, shrimp, salmon, sardines, tuna, herring, and mackerel. Fish liver oil is a highly concentrated source of vitamin D that can be taken as a dietary supplement if required.

During pregnancy, the recommended daily amount of vitamin D is 400 IU (international units). The body does store vitamin D, and overdose is possible. Excessive amounts of vitamin D can be harmful to the fetus, and use of an unprescribed supplement may not be prudent.

VITAMIN E

An adequate supply of vitamin E, which helps maintain the integrity of individual cell membranes, is related to normal growth patterns and the body's ability to respond to stress. Vitamin E is necessary for the body's digestion of polyunsaturated fats (vegetable oils). It is an antioxidant, which helps protect cells from damage caused during fat breakdown. Recent research suggests that the role vitamin E plays in helping the body deal with the effects of stress and aging may be even more important than previously understood.

The best food sources of vitamin E include wheat germ, wheat germ oil, sunflower oil, safflower oil, soybean oil, corn oil or corn oil margarine, almonds, hazelnuts, peanuts, peanut butter, peanut oil, cod liver oil, lobster, salmon, and whole grains.

Heat, oxygen, and freezing destroy vitamin E. If you are taking a vitamin supplement containing vitamin E, it's best to take it with a meal containing fats. Take your iron supplement at a different time—preferably eight hours earlier or later. If taken at the same time of day, certain iron supplements (ferrous sulphate, for example) destroy the effectiveness of vitamin E.

VITAMIN K

Vitamin K is necessary for blood clotting. The best source of this vitamin is within your own body, which can synthesize vitamin K from foodstuffs in the intestine. Dietary sources of vitamin K include leafy green vegetables such as kale, spinach, cabbage, turnip greens, lettuce, and asparagus. In addition to these vegetables, food sources of vitamin K include pork, whole wheat, oats, bran, tomatoes, carrots, and cauliflower.

After delivery, some caregivers recommend that a newborn receive an injection of vitamin K to prevent possible bleeding problems in the first few days until his or her intestines are well able to produce vitamin K on their own.

CALCIUM AND PHOSPHORUS

A good supply of calcium is important for the development of your baby's bones and teeth as well as for your health and general comfort during pregnancy. If your diet doesn't contain enough calcium, your baby will try to take what it needs from the stored supply in your bones. If you don't get enough calcium in your daily diet, you may be irritable and have trouble sleeping. Painful muscle cramps in the legs as well as pains in the uterus are also thought to be related to calcium deficiency.

Try to get the recommended 1,200 to 1,300 mg of calcium per day during pregnancy. Your body will be better able to absorb calcium in the presence of vitamin D and moderate amounts of fat. Fortified whole milk, therefore, would tend to be a more efficient source of calcium than lowfat or skim milk. There may, however, be other dietary reasons for you to prefer skim milk. If so, you might enhance calcium absorption by drinking the skim milk at a time when you are consuming another source of fat, such as a salad with an oily dressing or a piece of buttered toast.

Calcium can combine with certain other substances in foods and take forms that are less easily absorbed. The oxalic acid in spinach and beet greens, for example, decreases calcium absorption. Chocolate, candy, and other very concentrated carbohydrates may interfere with calcium absorption. Chocolate milk, for example, is likely to provide less readily usable calcium than a glass of plain milk. If you cannot or will not tolerate plain milk, however, it probably would be better to drink chocolate milk than none at all.

The following foods are good sources of calcium. Each of the amounts listed contains approximately 300 mg of calcium, the same amount as one eight-ounce (one-cup) glass of milk.

milk	8 ounces (one cup)
cottage cheese	12 ounces
natural (unprocessed) cheese	1⅓ ounces
dry milk powder	⅓ cup
ice cream	1½ cups
yogurt	1 cup
tofu (bean curd)	2 cakes, 2½″ × 2¾″ × 1″ each
salmon (canned, with bones)	½–⅔ cup (depends on brand)
ricotta cheese	½ cup

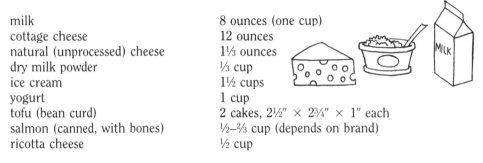

Adding dry powdered milk to hamburger, cereals, baked goods, pancakes, or blender concoctions will increase your intake of calcium. If you need an antacid, you might try Tums, which contains supplementary calcium. Consult your caregiver, although Tums is generally considered safe during pregnancy.

Calcium and the mineral phosphorus must be in balance for optimum health. If you follow the Food Guide Pyramid, you are likely to get the balance you need in your daily diet. The best dietary sources of phosphorus are meat, fish, poultry, and eggs. Milk and other dairy products are also high in phosphorus as well as in calcium.

An excess of phosphorus in relation to calcium may lead to a calcium deficiency. As you make your daily food choices using the Food Guide Pyramid, you can avoid an imbalance between calcium and phosphorus by paying careful attention to your intake of usable calcium to make sure it is sufficient. Soft drinks may contain large amounts of phosphorus (as the additive phosphoric acid), which can upset the body's calcium-phosphorus balance. Add this to your reasons for avoiding sodas or diet sodas during pregnancy.

Do not use bone meal or dolomite or any preparations containing them as calcium supplements while you are pregnant or nursing your baby. Samples of these mineral substances have been found to have a dangerously high lead content, which could cause serious harm to an unborn child or infant. Lead can cross the placenta and reach the fetus from the mother's body and can be transmitted to an infant through mother's milk.

IRON

During pregnancy, you will need an increased supply of iron to help produce extra hemoglobin, the oxygen-carrying substance of red blood cells. Extra iron is required for the production of hemoglobin in your expanding blood volume and in your baby's developing circulatory system. Anemia resulting from inadequate iron supply can reduce the baby's oxygen supply as well as cause extreme maternal fatigue (see page 34).

Your need for iron during pregnancy will probably double. For many women, it is very difficult to meet the increased requirement for iron solely by changes in diet. An iron supplement, therefore, is often recommended. You should, however, make an effort to eat iron-rich foods even if you do take an iron supplement. The body is generally better able to utilize iron from food sources.

Food sources of iron include beef or pork liver, kidney, veal, other meats, poultry, and fish, soybeans, oysters, dried fruit (apricots, peaches, prunes), prune juice, egg yolks, wheat germ, nuts, kidney beans, baked beans, chickpeas, and blackstrap molasses. Note that dried fruit and prune juice can relieve constipation as well as provide iron.

Your body will absorb iron more easily if you eat it with foods that contain a high level of vitamin C. You will, for example, be able to absorb more iron from your food if you have a glass of orange juice with your meal. Iron from animal source foods (meat, poultry, fish) tends to be more readily absorbed than iron from other sources. Iron may have been added to certain cereals and enriched breads that, although not the best source of this mineral, can add to your body's available iron supply.

If your care provider prescribes an iron supplement, be sure to take it as directed so it does the most good. It's usually best to take an iron supplement at a different time of day from your other prenatal vitamins.

SODIUM

Sodium, a mineral that is found in some quantity in nearly every food, is necessary to maintain the body's fluid balance. Table salt is 40 percent sodium. During pregnancy, a woman's body may need more sodium than usual because of the increase in the volume of her circulation. Many people, however, regularly consume far more sodium than they need. If you are one of those people, you may be advised to use the salt shaker sparingly and to make your food choices from items that do not have excessive amounts of added sodium. (See "Sodium Restrictions," page 63.)

Moderation in sodium intake is probably the most prudent course during pregnancy or any other time. Remember that some sodium occurs naturally in much of what you eat. If you follow the Food Guide Pyramid and eat a variety of foods from the different food groups, your daily diet is likely to contain more than enough sodium without special effort. Any salt you use in food preparation or at the table should be iodized or sea salt, to provide the trace mineral iodine in addition to sodium.

TRACE MINERALS

During pregnancy, the body requires a number of different minerals for maternal health and optimum fetal development. Minerals that are required in only small amounts are sometimes referred to as trace minerals. Although the amount of each one needed may be small, that does not mean it is insignificant.

The trace mineral iodine is necessary for healthy thyroid functioning. Severe iodine deficiency may be linked to abnormal fetal growth, but such deficiency is highly unlikely if you balance your food choices and use iodized salt or sea salt when you salt to taste in moderation. Shellfish is also an excellent dietary source of iodine.

Too much refined sugar, along with products made from highly processed and refined grains, may lead to inadequate chromium intake. Recent research suggests that a chromium deficiency may be associated with gestational diabetes. The best way to make sure you get enough chromium in your diet is to include as many whole grain products as you can in your bread, cereal, and pasta choices from the Food Guide Pyramid. Brewer's yeast is a supplementary source of chromium and numerous other nutrients. Other food sources of chromium include meats, mushrooms, and asparagus.

The trace mineral zinc is known to be important to protein synthesis and fetal growth. Zinc, like chromium, has been processed out of highly refined foods in the typical modern diet. The best food sources of zinc are oysters, herrings, and wheat germ. Zinc also is found in whole grains, beef, liver, peanuts, walnuts, almonds, eggs, sardines, and potatoes.

The trace mineral magnesium seems to have special importance during pregnancy. A deficiency of magnesium may be associated with preeclampsia or pregnancy-induced hypertension. Magnesium plays an important role in metabolism and protein synthesis. Food sources of magnesium include wheat germ, bran, whole grains, and nuts. Some leafy green vegetables may also provide magnesium.

Potassium is a trace mineral that is necessary for muscle activity, fluid balance, and protein synthesis. It works with other minerals, such as calcium, magnesium, and sodium to help prevent muscle cramps. Pregnant women may be more prone than others to cramp-causing mineral imbalances. An adequate supply of potassium can readily be obtained in your regular diet. The best food sources of potassium include potatoes, sweet potatoes or yams, squash, dried apricots, raisins, bananas, avocados, fish (flounder, salmon, sardines, cod, tuna, haddock, scallops), mushrooms, bran, and wheat germ. Leafy green vegetables are a source of potassium, as are most other meats, vegetables, and legumes.

The trace mineral selenium seems to play a role in disease prevention and stimulation of the immune system. Although some selenium is known to be necessary, too much of it can be toxic. Self-prescribed supplements of selenium (or any other substance) should be avoided. A protein-rich diet can provide all the selenium you need, because many high-protein foods also contain selenium. Among the best food sources of selenium are fish (especially tuna), whole wheat bread, liver and other organ meats, and rice.

Among the other trace minerals your body needs are copper, sulfur, manganese, and chloride. You would be unlikely to experience a deficiency of these minerals in a typical pregnancy diet.

If you follow the Food Guide Pyramid and eat a variety of foods from the different food groups, your daily diet is likely to contain the nutrients—including trace minerals—you need. As added insurance, many prenatal vitamin supplements also contain key minerals.

FOR YOUR NUTRITIONAL INFORMATION ____

The following section of *While Waiting* contains an alphabetical listing of nutrition-related topics about which many people have questions. Here you will find suggestions for dealing with a variety of topics, from food cravings and aversions, to artificial sweeteners, sodium restrictions, and fluid intake. Special guidelines for nutrition during pregnancy are provided here for teenagers, overweight women, underweight women, and vegetarians.

You or your prenatal caregiver should note here any topics that are especially important reading for your particular circumstances.

_____ page ____   _____ page ____

_____ page ____   _____ page ____

ADITIVES _____

Additives of one sort or another are included in most processed foods today. Some are safe, some are not. A number of them have not been tested thoroughly enough to determine if they are safe. During pregnancy, it's best to be very careful and plan your meals so additives that might be dangerous are avoided whenever possible.

This chart will help you do that.

Additive	Where Used	What to Do
Artificial food colorings, especially Blue No. 1, Blue No. 2, Citrus Red No. 2, Green No. 3, Red No. 3, and Yellow No. 6	Artificial coloring is found in a wide variety of products, from hot dogs to candy and baked goods.	Avoid. Most are poorly tested. Some are known to cause cancer in laboratory animals. Some are suspected of causing hyperactivity. All are unnecessary.
Artificial flavorings	Hundreds of different chemicals are used instead of natural flavors. They are identified only as "artificial flavor" on the label.	Avoid. These are often found in junk foods. The real thing may be more nutritious. Some artificial flavorings may cause hyperactivity. Foods containing artificial flavor are not necessary in your diet.
Artificial sweeteners	Acesulfame K, aspartame, or saccharin are used in diet sodas and foods.	Avoid these. Acesulfame K has not been well tested. Although some research indicates that aspartame is safe, it is suspected of causing brain damage in sensitive individuals and should not be used by people with PKU (see page 64). You can eat well without it. Saccharin is known to cause cancer in laboratory animals.
BHA (butylated hydroxyanisole) and BHT (butylated hydroxytoluene)	BHA and BHT are used in certain cereals, potato chips, oils, and chewing gum. They are antioxidants used to keep oils from becoming rancid.	Avoid. In a 1982 Japanese study, BHA caused cancer in rats, although other research suggests safety. Research on BHT is mixed. Both BHA and BHT can be replaced by safer substitutes.

Additive	Where Used	What to Do
Caffeine	Caffeine is a stimulant that occurs naturally in coffee, tea, and cocoa and is added to soft drinks.	Avoid or limit. Excessive use has been linked to miscarriage or birth defects, although recent research suggests moderate use may not be harmful in pregnancy. Caffeine may cause you to have trouble sleeping, and it has been linked to fibrocystic breast disease in some women.
MSG (monosodium glutamate)	MSG is a flavor enhancer often used in soups, poultry, seafood, stews, sauces, Chinese cooking, and many packaged convenience foods and specialty items.	Avoid. MSG in large amounts is known to injure brain cells of baby mice in lab experiments. MSG can cause headaches and "Chinese restaurant syndrome," a burning feeling and tightness in the face, head, neck, and arms.
Phosphoric acid; phosphates	These are used in certain baked goods, cured meats, dried potatoes, cereals, and sodas to provide flavor and prevent discoloration.	Although they are not toxic, their widespread use may lead to dietary imbalance that could result in osteoporosis.
Propyl gallate	This antioxidant is sometimes used in meat products, vegetable oils, potato sticks, some chicken soup stock, and chewing gum.	Avoid. Propyl gallate is not well tested. It is often used along with BHA and BHT. One long-term study suggested (but did not prove) a possible cancer link.
Quinine	Quinine is a flavoring used in tonic, quinine water, and bitter lemon.	Quinine is not well tested. It may cause birth defects. You aren't going to drink gin and tonic while you are pregnant anyway. Avoid.
Sodium nitrite; sodium nitrate	These are used to preserve, color, and flavor such meats as bacon, ham, hot dogs, corned beef, and lunch meats.	Avoid. Especially in fried bacon, these can cause formation of nitrosamines, which can cause cancer. Many products containing these additives are high in fat content and should be avoided for that reason as well.

Additive	Where Used	What to Do
Sulfur dioxide; sodium bisulfite	These preservative and bleaching agents are found in sliced fruit, dried fruit, some "fresh" shrimp, dried potatoes, wine, and grape juice.	Avoid. Sulfiting agents prevent discoloration of dried or sliced fruit, shrimp, and some processed potatoes. They retard bacterial growth in wine. They also destroy vitamin B_1 and can cause severe allergic reactions (even death) in sensitive individuals.

SOURCE: "Chemical Cuisine," published by Center for Science in the Public Interest. (You can order "Chemical Cuisine" as a poster or a pocket-sized slide chart from: Center for Science in the Public Interest, 1875 Connecticut Avenue, Suite 300, Washington, D.C. 20009. Telephone [202] 332-9110.)

Watch carefully for the additives listed in the above table and avoid them if you can. Many additives, however, are safe and necessary. When you read a label, don't be fooled by long names that are hard to pronounce. Current government regulations may require an ingredient to be listed by its technical chemical name. Some such items have been known by other names and used safely for years.

AVERSIONS

During pregnancy, especially in the first trimester, when nausea and vomiting may be a problem, some women develop strong aversions to certain foods. If this happens to you, you'll probably have to avoid the item in self-defense. There's no point in trying to swallow something you can't stomach even if it would be good for you under normal circumstances. Substitute small portions of things you can tolerate.

Use the Food Guide Pyramid to make certain that what you do eat provides the needed nutritional balance. If you can't keep any food down or you find that your aversions are so widespread that you are unable to choose from each of the food groups, consult your care provider.

CAFFEINE

Some research has suggested a relationship between excessive consumption of caffeine during pregnancy and birth defects. Although small to moderate amounts are probably not harmful, you may wish to be on the safe side and limit your intake of coffee, tea, cola, and other items containing caffeine. Because some over-the-counter or prescription drugs may also contain caffeine, you should check out the ingredients with your pharmacist or prenatal care provider before taking any during pregnancy.

Experts differ on the extent to which caffeine may be a danger during pregnancy. Recent research suggests that moderate daily amounts of caffeine—what would be found in three cups of coffee, six to seven cups of tea, or eight cola drinks, for example— are not related to miscarriage or birth defects as once suspected.

Caffeine is a stimulant, and it does cross the placenta to your baby. If you feel the need for a cup of coffee or even two in the morning to get you going, that's probably all right. But don't overdo it. The cumulative effects of frequent coffee or cola breaks during the day could cause trouble and aren't worth the risk. Furthermore, the person who drinks too much coffee, tea, or cola may tend to neglect more nutritious beverages, such as fruit juices, milk, or soups.

CALORIES

The Food Guide Pyramid is designed to help you make healthful food choices without having to count the calories in every bite you take. If you choose wisely from each of the food groups and try to minimize added sugars and fats, you are likely to obtain the nutrients and the energy you need.

If you would like to know approximately how many calories you should be getting in a typical day, there is a formula you can use as a guide. Begin with the number that represents your prepregnancy weight. If your life-style involves only light physical activity, multiply your weight by 12. If you are moderately active, multiply your weight by 15. If you are very active, multiply your weight by 20. To whatever number you get, add 300 extra calories just for being pregnant. The result is likely to be a sensible guide for your daily caloric intake.

CHOLESTEROL

Cholesterol is a fatlike substance present in animal tissues, including human blood. Dietary cholesterol and saturated fats can team up to raise the artery-clogging level of your blood cholesterol and increase the risk of serious health problems, including heart disease and stroke. Pregnancy does not, however, intensify the risk. In other words, you should minimize your intake of saturated fats and cholesterol for your general health, not because you happen to be pregnant.

Many nutritionists recommend that intake of dietary cholesterol be limited to an average of 300 mg per day or less. You probably can do that by following the Food Guide Pyramid and keeping your intake of total fats within the suggested levels. If you choose wisely and eat a variety of foods from the different food groups, cholesterol is not likely to be a serious problem.

To cut down your intake of saturated fats and cholesterol, use skim or lowfat dairy products and fish or lean meats in preference to cuts that contain more fat. If you must use added fats or oils (the tip of the Pyramid) in food preparation, avoid animal fats (lard, butter, meat drippings, bacon grease) and tropical oils with unsaturated fats (palm oil and coconut oil). It's best to use olive oil or canola oil (monounsaturated fats). Safflower oil, corn oil, soybean oil, and sunflower oil (polyunsaturated fats) are also acceptable choices, although not quite as good as olive oil. In your total for the day, remember to count any fats or oils consumed in processed foods or used for cooking.

Don't be misled by packaged products that proclaim to be "cholesterol free." Some of these never had cholesterol to begin with, so the claim is not news. Being cholesterol free, furthermore, does not mean the product is nutritious or good for you, although it may be. Before you fall for the low-cholesterol claim, make sure the product has at least some needed nutrients and isn't too high in other kinds of fat or added sugars.

CRAVINGS

Some women develop cravings for one or more particular food items during pregnancy, although many women do not. Ice cream and pickles, for example, seem to be a staple of pregnancy eating tales. Also among the foods that some women have reported craving are fish, certain fruits, milk, candy, and other sweets. There is no widely accepted explanation for food cravings, although their existence has been well documented.

If you develop a sudden urge for a certain food, go ahead and indulge your craving if that food provides energy or an essential nutrient such as calcium. Check out where the food you crave belongs on the Food Guide Pyramid. If your craving persists to the point where eating the desired food prevents you from obtaining other essential nutrients, try to bring your daily menu back into a reasonable balance.

Some pregnant women develop a condition called "pica" in which they crave and attempt to consume nonfood items such as dirt, gravel, ashes, paint chips, or ice. If you find yourself eating nonfood substances, consult your care provider before you cause harm to yourself or your unborn baby.

FIBER

Adequate amounts of dietary fiber (roughage) are needed to promote general health and to prevent constipation. If you choose wisely from the different food groups in the Food Guide Pyramid, your diet is likely to contain enough fiber-rich foods.

You can ensure adequate fiber intake by using whole grains instead of products made from refined flour and including plenty of raw or minimally cooked vegetables and fruits in your diet. Dried fruits are an excellent source of dietary fiber, as are legumes and nuts.

To maximize dietary fiber from a fiber-rich food, minimize processing and cooking. A raw apple, for example, has more fiber than does applesauce. Raw or lightly steamed broccoli has more fiber than cooked broccoli pureed into cream of broccoli soup. Added bran or wheat germ will increase the fiber content of cereals and baked goods.

Because fiber may interfere with the body's ability to absorb calcium, try not to take in your main sources of calcium at the same time of day you consume extremely fiber-rich foods.

FLUIDS

During pregnancy, you should drink at least two quarts (eight to ten glasses) of liquid a day. In addition to water, good sources of fluid are unsweetened fruit and vegetable juices. Avoid such drinks as fruit punches and ades, which have a lot of sugar added and provide unnecessary calories. Remember that the tip of the Food Guide Pyramid advises you to use added sweets sparingly. Presugared drinks fall into this category. Alcoholic beverages, which under different circumstances would be counted along with the added sugars at the Pyramid's tip, should not be used at all during pregnancy.

You should avoid carbonated beverages because they have little or no nutritional value and they produce gas that may make you uncomfortable. Regular sodas are very high in calories. Diet sodas, on the other hand, contain potentially dangerous additives such as aspartame or saccharin. Diet sodas sometimes have more sodium and caffeine than do regular sodas.

The bubbles in carbonated beverages increase the surface area of food available for exposure to digestive enzymes, thus enabling the enzymes to act more rapidly and completely. While this may cause you to derive more energy from certain foods, it may also increase the practical impact of the caloric intake. In other words, carbonation has the potential disadvantage of helping empty calories affect you more quickly.

FOLIC ACID

Folic acid (also referred to as folacin or folate) is one of the B vitamins. Folic acid, which plays a role in cell growth and the development of DNA and RNA, is an especially important nutrient during pregnancy. The U.S. recommended daily allowance of folic acid for the general population is 0.4 milligrams, and a woman's need for this B vitamin doubles to 0.8 milligrams during pregnancy. Women with an inadequacy of folic acid are at increased risk of having a baby with neural tube defects. Recent research has demonstrated that the incidence of neural tube defects can be reduced by at least half if women take folic acid during the early weeks of pregnancy.

Folic acid gets its name from the word *folium*, the Latin word for leaf, a fact that can help you remember that the best dietary source of folic acid is leafy green vegetables such as spinach, collard greens, broccoli, romaine lettuce, brussels sprouts, or asparagus. Use raw vegetables for salads and snacks, or cook minimally by steaming or microwaving. Like other B vitamins, folic acid is fragile and easily lost during food storage, preparation, and cooking. Other dietary sources of folic acid include oranges, orange juice, whole grains, lentils, and peanuts. Some ready-to-eat breakfast cereals are fortified with folic acid, and proposals have been made to add folic acid to bread and other grain products. It's important to read product labels carefully.

Because folic acid plays such a significant role in fetal cell development right from the start of pregnancy, some care providers recommend that women take supplementary vitamins containing folic acid even before conception.

OBESITY

No matter how overweight a woman may be before she becomes pregnant, she should still gain weight during pregnancy. Even if a woman is extremely obese, she must nourish her unborn child with nutrients from fresh foods rather than from her fat reserves.

A fetus cannot be adequately nourished by the mother's stored fat. In fact, breakdown of the mother's fat reserves may even cause the fetus harm. Burning of stored fat can release potentially dangerous chemicals called ketones into the mother's bloodstream. The fetus also may be exposed to toxic substances such as polychlorinated biphenyls (PCBs) that may be stored in body fat and released as the fat cells break down.

It's very important for an overweight woman to use the principles of the Food Guide

Pyramid in planning her food intake. She should keep to the suggested balance of various types of food and avoid packaged diet products for weight loss or food fads. If she has been on a reducing diet prior to pregnancy, she should stop the calorie curtailment as soon as she knows she is pregnant. If she is more than 20 percent over her ideal weight, however, she may gain weight at a slightly slower rate than what would normally be recommended. An extremely overweight woman may be advised to strive for a weight gain of only twenty pounds. Any smaller gain, however, is likely to be at the baby's expense.

SODIUM RESTRICTIONS

At one time, it was thought that the typical swelling of legs, hands, or feet during pregnancy was related to excess sodium intake and that routine salt restriction could help control such swelling. That view is no longer considered correct. Sodium restriction does not cure edema (swelling), and severe restriction may actually cause harm. (See pages 33–4 for suggestions on dealing with edema.)

Although severe salt restrictions are no longer recommended during pregnancy, it's best for you and your entire family to avoid excessive amounts of sodium at any time. Try to limit your intake of excessively salty foods. Skip salted snack food such as potato chips, crackers, pretzels, crisps, or salted peanuts, some of which may have excessive amounts of fat as well as too much sodium. Limit olives, pickles, soy sauce, and MSG.

Most canned or packaged foods contain added sodium in one form or another. Bouillion cubes, canned soups, and soup packages tend to have high amounts of added sodium. Read labels carefully when you buy. Ingredients are listed in descending order by quantity. The closer salt or a form of sodium is to the beginning of the list, the more there is relative to the other ingredients.

SWEETENERS (ARTIFICIAL)

The tip of the Food Guide Pyramid counsels you to use sweets sparingly. Substituting artificial sweeteners such as acesulfame K, aspartame, or saccharin for sugars may not be a wise substitution, especially during pregnancy.

Acesulfame K, marketed commercially as Sunette or Sweet One, was approved by the FDA in 1988 for use as a sugar substitute and as an ingredient in beverage mixes, gelatin desserts, puddings, and nondairy creamers. The types of products that contain acesulfame K have little if any place in a nutritious food plan. Testing of this sweetener may have been inadequate, and there is really no reason to risk using it during pregnancy.

Aspartame, approved in 1981 for sale in the United States, is a widely used artificial sweetener. Aspartame is marketed as a sugar substitute under the trade name Equal. As the food additive NutraSweet, it is found in a wide variety of products, from diet sodas to breakfast foods and packaged desserts. Although aspartame is popular and generally regarded as safe, some researchers have suggested that high doses of the additive may be associated with problems ranging from headaches, dizziness, and subtle brain changes to mental retardation.

Those with a condition known as PKU (phenylketonuria), an inability to metabolize phenylalanine, one of two amino acids that make up aspartame, should not use aspartame. Products containing the additive carry a warning label to this effect. Some scientists believe that excessive use of aspartame by a woman who carries the PKU trait even if she does not have the disease might place her unborn child at risk of mental retardation. This view is disputed, however, by the product's manufacturers and the FDA.

Aspartame's effects vary with individual sensitivity to the substance. Pregnant women and their babies may be more susceptible to the effects of aspartame than nonpregnant adults would be. During pregnancy you probably should avoid products containing aspartame. The amount of the additive, if any, that might be a safe dose for an unborn child is not known with certainty.

Saccharin is used in certain diet soft drinks, packaged diet foods, and desserts. It is sold as a sugar substitute under the brand name Sweet 'N Low. Although saccharin has been marketed for nearly a century in this country, there has been relatively little research on its safety for use during pregnancy. Studies have linked saccharin to cancer in laboratory animals. In addition to saccharin's potential health hazards, the artificial sweetener does not seem to be significantly effective as an aid to weight loss. There simply is no reason a pregnant woman should use saccharin. There are a number of reasons she should not use it.

SWEETENERS (SUGARS) _____

Although added sugar may make certain food items taste more pleasing to you, sugar does not contain nutrients that will benefit you or your developing baby. Sugar provides empty calories, about sixteen of them per teaspoonful. Any quick energy high you might get from sweets probably isn't worth the cost.

It's important for you to avoid getting too many calories from sugars. Excessive intake of sugars can crowd out essential nutrients you and your baby need. Using artificial sweeteners instead of sugar may be hazardous and should be avoided. Does that mean you must avoid any indulgence of a sweet tooth during pregnancy? Not necessarily. A reasonable approach for most women would be to follow the Food Guide Pyramid's suggestion to use sweets sparingly.

If you want a bit of sugar on your cereal, some jam on your toast, a spoonful of sugar in a cup of tea, or an occasional sweet dessert, you need not feel guilty. Just make sure you aren't filling up on empty calories at the expense of the nutrients you need from the various food groups. If you are gaining too much weight, think about the tip of the Pyramid. Make sure you aren't overloading your diet with added sugars, fats, or oils.

To help you use sweets sparingly, it's not enough to count the sugar you use in food preparation or in your tea. You also have to know which packaged foods in your food choices contain added sugars. You have to read labels. Remember that sugar by any other name—sucrose, fructose, glucose, dextrose, honey, raw sugar, turbinado sugar, brown sugar, molasses, corn syrup, high-fructose corn syrup, maple syrup—is still sugar, a simple carbohydrate without significant nutritional value.

You might be surprised to find out how many different food products contain one or more forms of sugar. Sugar is not confined to obvious sweets such as cookies, cakes, and candy. You'll also find it in some brands of ketchup, barbecue sauce, spaghetti sauce, salad dressing, peanut butter, cereal, nondairy creamer, soup, gravy, bread crumb mixes, hot dogs, and lunch meats, among other things. Fruit drinks and ades may have the equivalent of as much as a teaspoon of sugar per ounce of drink. A serving of canned fruit in heavy syrup may have four teaspoons of added sugar. Depending on the brand, eight ounces of flavored or fruit yogurt may have from five to seven teaspoons of added sugar.

Don't be misled into thinking certain forms of sugar, such as honey or brown sugar, are nutritionally more virtuous than refined white sugar. The bottom line is that sugar is sugar (except, perhaps, for blackstrap molasses, which does contain some iron, calcium, potassium, and B vitamins, especially vitamin B_6).

TEENAGERS

A teenager who is still growing has significantly greater nutritional needs than a fully mature adult would have. For a teenager, the consequences of careless eating during pregnancy may be more severe. A pregnant teenager must eat carefully, not only for the needs of her developing baby, but also for her own growth and development. She will need increased amounts of protein, calcium, iron, and a number of vitamins.

No pregnant woman should diet to lose weight, and a weight-loss diet would be especially risky for a pregnant teenager and her unborn baby. To avoid having a low birth weight baby, a young person who is still growing might have to gain more weight during pregnancy than she would if her own body were already fully mature.

Although you must eat to nourish your own growing body and that of your baby, this doesn't mean you should overeat. Your prenatal care provider can help you work out the right eating plan for you. Ask whether you should strive for a somewhat larger weight gain than the typically recommended twenty-four to thirty pounds. If so, you may wish to follow the suggestions for underweight women on pages 65–6.

Be sure to eat breakfast, even if you don't feel like doing so. If you can't stand traditional breakfast foods, substitute something else that's nutritious. A tuna fish sandwich on whole wheat bread, for example, will do you and your baby as much good in the morning as it would at lunchtime. If plain milk isn't one of your favorite beverages, you can increase your calcium intake by adding nonfat milk powder to things you do like to eat and drink.

If you are a pregnant teenager, it's important to become informed. Your baby's well-being will be directly influenced by what you eat. Adolescent girls tend to have the poorest nutritional habits of any age group, but pregnancy is a special reason for you to avoid unhealthful eating habits, even if your friends do otherwise. Avoid junk foods and fad diets. If you work at it, you should be able to fill in the Food Guide Pyramid with many foods you will enjoy as you nourish yourself and your baby.

UNDERWEIGHT WOMEN

A woman who is significantly underweight prior to pregnancy must take special care to avoid having a baby of low birth weight. She should try to gain the extra pounds she needs to achieve the recommended weight for her height and build in addition to the twenty-four to thirty pounds usually suggested. A woman who is ten to twelve pounds underweight at conception, for example, may be advised to strive for a weight gain of up to forty pounds.

Needing to gain extra weight is not, however, an excuse to pig out on junk foods or fattening substances that are not nutritious. The principles of the Food Guide Pyramid still hold. If you need to gain more weight, you should maintain a nutritious balance while increasing your caloric intake. You might try eating somewhat smaller meals, but twice as many of them during the day. Substitute whole milk for skim milk. Add nonfat milk powder to sauces, gravy, soups, casseroles, meatloaf, pancakes, and baked goods. Eat an extra slice of bread or toast, and don't skimp on the jam. Indulge in a nutritious dessert, such as ice cream or ice milk, pudding, a malted, or a shake. Try a fruit topping on your ice cream or just eat an extra piece of fresh fruit. Enjoy.

VEGETARIANISM

If you are a vegetarian and intend to continue your dietary practices during pregnancy, you will have to plan your menus with care to ensure that you meet not only your nutritional needs but those of your developing baby. How easy this will be depends, in part, on the type of vegetarian regimen you follow. If, for example, you do not eat meat but do eat fish and seafood, the Food Guide Pyramid will work as easily for you as it would for anyone else.

If you avoid meat, poultry, and fish but do eat eggs, milk, and other dairy products (lacto-ovo vegetarianism), you can follow the Food Guide Pyramid to a healthful diet. If you eat dairy products but no eggs (lacto vegetarianism), you still will be able to use the Food Guide Pyramid with relative ease. Because eggs and milk are complete proteins, either will combine with incomplete proteins to provide the needed amino acids. You may require an iron supplement and/or prenatal vitamins.

If you are a strict vegan—a person who eats no animal products, including eggs, milk, and other dairy products—it will be extremely difficult for you to meet all of your nutritional needs without some supplementation. You will have to be certain that your food choices provide sufficient protein. You will have to know which incomplete proteins complement each other to form complete proteins, and plan your meals accordingly. (See page 49.)

Because animal products are the source of vitamin B_{12}, a strict vegan would need supplementation of this nutrient during pregnancy. Without supplementation, a vegan diet is unlikely to provide sufficient amounts of a number of other key nutrients, such as folic acid, iron, and zinc.

Although it is possible for a vegan to get enough calcium, protein, and calories through a strict vegetarian diet alone, it is not easy. Without dairy products or eggs, a very large volume of food would be needed to ensure protein complementation, needed nutrients, and sufficient caloric intake. To give her baby the best possible start in life, a pregnant vegan may wish to consider adding certain items (such as dairy products, eggs, or even fish) to her diet until after her baby is born.

Discuss with your prenatal care provider any dietary practices you follow that might make it more difficult to ensure optimum nutrition for you and your baby. If food choice changes or supplementation are necessary, it's best to find out sooner rather than later.

VITAMINS (MEGADOSES)

Some people today take massive doses of certain vitamins because they believe there are certain health or nutrition benefits in doing so. No matter what your personal views might be about taking megadoses of vitamins, however, pregnancy is a time to avoid this practice. While your body may be able to cope comfortably with large amounts of various vitamins, this same quantity could damage your baby.

VITAMINS (PRENATAL SUPPLEMENTS)

Most care providers feel that prenatal vitamins are added insurance that you and your baby are getting all the vitamins you need. It is true that most vitamin needs can be met through a well-balanced diet. It's often difficult, however, to tell for sure what you are getting from your food alone. Many vitamins can be destroyed or weakened during food processing or preparation. A vitamin supplement formulated for use during pregnancy is an extra safeguard.

If you are taking supplementary vitamins prescribed by your caregiver, keep in mind that these are not a substitute for eating well. You can't swallow the pill and skip the meal.

WIC PROGRAM

If you cannot afford all of the nutritious foods you should have to keep healthy during pregnancy, you may be eligible for WIC, a Special Supplemental Food Program for Women, Infants, and Children. The WIC program provides a monthly check that can be used at grocery stores to purchase nutritious foods such as milk, eggs, juice, cheese, cereal, peanut butter, and legumes.

If your income is limited and you are having trouble purchasing the foods you need to follow the Food Guide Pyramid, ask your care provider or your local social services department about WIC.

EXERCISES WHILE WAITING _____

The following pages contain exercises designed to improve posture, strengthen important muscles, relieve tension and pressure, and help you relax. These exercises can make you more comfortable during pregnancy while they help prepare your body for labor and delivery. Many of them will also be useful after your baby is born as you work to restore your body to its prepregnancy fitness.

Begin these exercises gradually—twice will do for each exercise the first time around. Work up to five repetitions, or even ten or more, but do it gradually. Remember to keep within the bounds of what is comfortable for you. If a particular exercise causes you discomfort or pain, stop.

Exercises done lying on the back may be inadvisable in late pregnancy (from about the fifth month on). Ask your care provider if there are any special cautions you should observe at this time.

If more than one exercise is suggested for the same purpose, you don't need to do them all. Pick one that suits you best, or alternate for variety. The important thing is to do what makes sense for you.

PELVIC FLOOR EXERCISES _____

These are perhaps the most important exercises you can do to prepare you body for labor and delivery and for a rapid postpartum recovery. A strong and elastic pelvic floor can reduce or prevent problems such as sagging organs or leaking urine. Because these exercises strengthen the muscles used in intercourse and orgasm, they also may increase sexual enjoyment.

Pelvic floor exercises are easily and conveniently done almost anytime or anywhere. Try them while you're in a car or train, watching TV, brushing teeth, talking on the telephone, doing things around the house, waiting around, making love, or just doing nothing. You'll find these exercises very helpful in promoting healing and restoring muscle tone after your baby is born.

KEGEL EXERCISE #1

You can do this exercise in any position—lying down, sitting, or standing. Your legs should be slightly apart.

Tighten and then release the muscles around your vagina. Work up to doing this one hundred or more times a day. (Note that twenty times five, or ten times ten will be more effective and less tiring than one hundred times without stopping.)

Here are two techniques to help you get the feel of this exercise.

1. Place your hand over your pubic bones. Imagine you are trying to contract your vaginal muscles as far up as your hand.
2. Try this exercise while urinating. If you can start and stop the flow of urine at will, you've got it.

KEGEL EXERCISE #2

Tighten and release the vaginal muscles as in Kegel #1. This time, however, you will do it more slowly. Tighten the muscles slowly as you count to six (or time yourself using a clock with a second hand). Then slowly relax to a count of four. Then tighten and hold again for six seconds. Relax for four. Begin with a minute. Work up to five minutes at a time, several times a day. Breathe normally as you do this exercise. Resist the temptation to hold your breath as you count.

BETTER POSTURE AND COMFORT _____

Here are simple exercises to improve your posture while sitting and standing. You will look better and feel more comfortable if you have good posture. Skip the tailor sitting exercises if they cause pain in the pubic bone area. You may already have separation here, and in that case you shouldn't continue this particular set of exercises.

BACK FLATTENING #1

Stand with your back to the wall and your feet a few inches away. Your head, shoulders, and buttocks should be touching the wall. Stand tall and straighten your neck and your lower back muscles. Count to ten. Relax. Do it again. Work up to ten times.

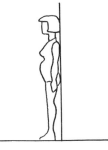

BACK FLATTENING #2

Lie on the floor on your back, with your toes pointing up. Straighten your back and pretend you are trying to push yourself—still flat on your back—straight through the floorboards. Count to ten. Relax. Do it again. Work up to ten times.

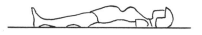

BACK FLATTENING #3

Lie on the floor on your back as in exercise #2. Keeping your arms straight and on the floor at all times, raise your hands until your arms are straight above your head. Then bring them slowly back to your sides. (Some of us learned the movements for this exercise as children making "angels in the snow.") Repeat ten times.

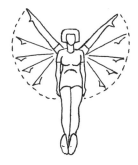

TAILOR SITTING #1

Sit on the floor with your legs crossed just over the ankles. Your back should be slightly rounded. This position will help to stretch the muscles of your inner thighs and get you used to relaxing your pelvic floor with your legs apart. Try sitting in this position while reading or watching TV.

TAILOR SITTING #2

While sitting in the tailor position, hold your hands one under each knee. Press your knees to the floor while providing pressure in the other direction with your hands.

TAILOR SITTING #3

Sit on the floor with the soles of your feet together. Slowly pull your heels as close to your body as you can comfortably.

EXERCISES FOR LEGS

These exercises will help relieve circulatory problems in your legs. They are useful for dealing with discomfort from swelling, varicose veins, and cramps.

SWINGING FEET

Draw large circles in the air with your toes. Rotate your ankles and feet to draw the circles, but try not to move your legs. You can do both feet at once or one foot at a time. Do some circles from left to right and some from right to left.

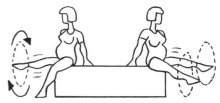

MORE SWINGING FEET

If drawing plain circles in the air with your feet gets boring, try making letters with your toes. Write a letter of the alphabet or an entire word while moving only your feet and ankles, not your legs. You'll probably find it easier to move one foot at a time. You can do this to keep your circulation going anytime you are sitting down.

LEG LIFTS

Lie on your back with bent knees and your feet flat on the floor. One leg at a time, pull your knee up toward your shoulder. Then straighten your leg and point it toward the ceiling. Without bending your leg, lower it smoothly and gently to the floor. Return to your starting position. Repeat with the other leg. Do not try to do this exercise with both legs at once. ___

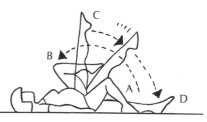

EXERCISES FOR THE UPPER BACK ___

These exercises will help prevent and relieve aches and tension in the neck, upper back, and shoulders.

ARM STRETCH

Stand up and keep your feet flat on the floor. Stretch one arm at a time, reaching as high as you can. Stretch one arm and then the other. Work up to ten or more times.

BACK STRETCH

Lie flat on your back on the floor. Point your toes to the ceiling. Stretch first one side and then the other. Pull your toes up toward your shoulders and push away with your heels. Work up to ten or more times.

HEAD ROLLING

You can sit on a chair or the edge of a bed for this exercise. Or, if you prefer, try sitting on the floor in the tailor position. Relax your neck and shoulder muscles. Roll your head around and around. Work up to five times clockwise and five times counterclockwise. Be sure to keep your neck as relaxed as possible and let the weight of your head roll it around.

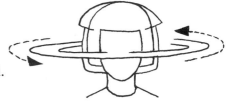

SHOULDER ROTATION #1

Extend your arms straight out from your shoulders. Make circles with your arms. Do five in one direction and five in the other. Stretch your arms way out straight and feel the muscles in your shoulder blades as they work.

SHOULDER ROTATION #2

Put one hand on each shoulder and point your elbows straight out from your sides. Make circles with your elbows just as you did with your arms straight in the previous exercise. Both shoulder rotation exercises can be done while sitting in the tailor position.

EXERCISES FOR ABDOMINAL MUSCLES _____

Before doing the exercises to strengthen your abdominal muscles, follow the procedures suggested below to check for separation of these muscles. If your muscles have separated, you should do the exercise designed to prevent further separation. If not, you can safely go on to the more strenuous exercises that follow.

SEPARATION CHECK

Your abdominal muscles are arranged in two bands. During pregnancy, these muscles may separate at the seam. Here's how to check for separation. (You need your clothes off for this one.) Lie on your back. Bend your knees and keep your feet flat on the floor. Raise your head and shoulders slowly until your neck is about eight inches off the floor. If you can see a hollow (in early pregnancy or postpartum) or a bulge (in late pregnancy) your abdominal muscles are weak. Do the exercise that follows to help avoid further separation.

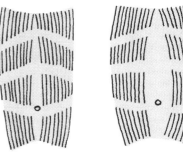

EXERCISE FOR SEPARATED MUSCLES

Lie on your back with your knees bent and your feet flat on the floor. Cross your hands and place them on your abdomen. Push the sides of your abdomen toward the center. Raise your head as you did in the separation check, but this time stop just before the point where you would see the hollow or the bulge. Work up to doing this at least five times, twice a day.

BACK ROUNDING

If you begin this exercise early in your pregnancy, you'll probably find it helpful. It's a difficult one to begin later on, however, so if you have trouble, skip it. Do not use this exercise if your abdominal muscles have separated.

Lie on your back with bent knees and your feet flat on the floor. Rest your chin on your chest. Reach for your knees with your hands. As you exhale slowly, raise your head and shoulders as far as you can with your waist still on the floor. Work up to five times, twice a day.

BREATHE IN, BREATHE OUT, AND BLOW

Lie on your back with your feet flat on the floor and your knees bent. Put a pillow under your head if you wish. Breathe in through your nose and let your abdomen rise gently. Breathe out through your nose and let your abdomen return to its normal position. Now, without taking another breath, blow out gently through your mouth as long as you can. You should feel your abdominal muscles tighten. Work up to doing this ten times.

PELVIC ROCK #1 (ANGRY CAT)

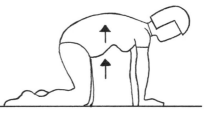

Get down on your hands and knees. Keep your knees a little bit apart and your back flat. Resist the temptation to hollow the small of your back. Make sure your hands are directly under your shoulders, not farther forward or back. Tighten up your buttock muscles and pull your hips in toward your chin. At the same time, tighten your abdominal muscles and arch your back like an angry cat. Hold this position for a few seconds, then relax. Work up to ten times or more.

PELVIC ROCK #2

Lie on the floor with your knees bent and the soles of your feet flat on the floor. Flatten your back to the floor while at the same time pulling in your abdominal muscles. Be sure to keep your buttocks on the floor while you are pushing down with your back. Work up to ten times or more.

PELVIC ROCK #3 (HULA HOOP)

Follow the same moves as in Pelvic Rock #2. As you are keeping your buttocks on the floor and pushing down with your back, make circular motions with your hips on the floor as if you were using a hula hoop.

WHEELBARROW

This exercise may help relieve pelvic pain caused by the pressure of your baby. You need your partner's help for this one. Lie on your back with your head on a pillow and your knees bent. Your partner should kneel close to your side, or he may squat with one leg on each side and lean over you if he prefers. He should hold your hips as if he is holding the handles of a wheelbarrow. He should slowly lift your hips, hold them to a count of three, and then lower them gently.

RELAXATION TECHNIQUES

Knowing how to relax completely is something you will find very useful when you are anxious or physically uncomfortable. The kind of relaxing we are talking about is not simply the absence of activity. It is a conscious release of tension as you concentrate on one part of your body after another. To learn to do this requires practice, and it may help if you do your relaxing as a regular part of your exercise routine.

RELAXING #1

Choose a position that is comfortable for you. You may sit, stand, or lie down. Let go of tension starting at the top of your head. Concentrate on one part of your body after another in turn until you reach your feet. Take as long as you need and breathe naturally. For variety, you can begin at your toes and work up. Follow this with Relaxing #2 below.

RELAXING #2

Here's a shortcut to relaxing your body. Concentrate on and relax each of these four areas in turn:

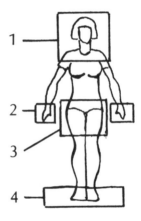

1. face, neck, and shoulders
2. hands
3. bottom and thighs
4. feet

When you need to relax in a hurry, this shortcut to total relaxation may help you.

FOR YOUR INFORMATION

ACNE AND ACCUTANE
ADDICTIVE DRUGS
AEROBIC EXERCISE
AIDS
ALCOHOL
ALPHA FETOPROTEIN (AFP) TEST
ALTERNATIVE BIRTH SETTINGS
AMNIOCENTESIS
AMNIOTOMY
AUTOMOBILE SAFETY
BATHS
BIOPHYSICAL PROFILE
BONDING
BREASTFEEDING PREPARATION
BREECH PRESENTATION
CAESAREAN DELIVERY
CHLAMYDIA
CHORIONIC VILLUS SAMPLING (CVS)
CONTRACTION STRESS TEST
DENTAL CARE
DIABETES
DISABILITY BENEFITS
DIURETICS
DOUCHING
DOWN SYNDROME
ECTOPIC PREGNANCY
ELECTRONIC FETAL MONITORING
EMPLOYMENT
ENEMA
EPIDURAL ANESTHESIA
EPISIOTOMY
EXERCISE
FORCEPS DELIVERY
GENETIC COUNSELING
GENITAL HERPES
GESTATIONAL DIABETES

HOUSEHOLD HAZARDS
INDUCED LABOR
KICK COUNT
LEBOYER DELIVERY
LOVEMAKING
LYME DISEASE
MARIJUANA
MEDICATIONS (FOR LABOR AND
    DELIVERY)
MISCARRIAGE
NONSTRESS TEST
OVER-THE-COUNTER MEDICATIONS
PREECLAMPSIA (TOXEMIA)
PREGNANCY LOSS
PREP
PREPARED CHILDBIRTH
PRESCRIPTION DRUGS AND MEDICINES
Rh-NEGATIVE MOTHERS
RUBELLA
SAUNAS AND HOT TUBS
SEXUALLY TRANSMITTED DISEASES
SIBLING PARTICIPATION
SMOKING
SPORTS
TAMPONS
TOXIC SUBSTANCES
TOXOPLASMOSIS
TRAVEL
TWINS
ULTRASOUND
VAGINAL BIRTH AFTER CAESAREAN
    (VBAC)
WEIGHT
WORKPLACE HAZARDS
X RAYS
BOOKS FOR YOUR INFORMATION

FOR YOUR INFORMATION

The following section of *While Waiting* contains an alphabetical listing of topics about which many people have questions. Here you will find guidelines for activities and personal health care during pregnancy. This section also contains brief explanations of certain medical procedures and terms. If you have further questions about any of the listed items or questions about things not included here, BE SURE TO ASK.

You or your prenatal caregiver should note here any topics that are especially important reading for your particular circumstances.

_____ page ____	_____ page ____
_____ page ____	_____ page ____
_____ page ____	_____ page ____

ACNE AND ACCUTANE

Accutane is a prescription medication used to treat severe cystic acne. Accutane, which is very effective in relieving facial acne scars, is known to cause serious birth defects if used by a pregnant woman. Use of Accutane during pregnancy can lead to a twenty-five-fold increase in the chances of having a severely malformed baby. Among the problems associated with Accutane are babies born with abnormalities of the brain and central nervous system, the ears, face, heart, and the thymus gland, along with some degree of mental retardation.

Before beginning a course of acne treatment using Accutane, a pregnancy test to make sure you are not pregnant is essential. If you know you are pregnant or you plan to become pregnant in the near future, do not use Accutane, even if it has been prescribed for you in the past by a dermatologist or other physician. You should also avoid megadoses of supplementary vitamin A, the substance from which Accutane is derived (see pages 50–1 and 67).

ADDICTIVE DRUGS

The placenta does not protect the fetus from the mother's use of drugs such as cocaine, crack cocaine, LSD, heroin, alcohol, caffeine, and nicotine. These substances all cross the placenta and have the potential to cause serious harm. Use of such drugs during pregnancy has been associated with various birth defects, including brain damage and physical abnormalities.

A woman's use of cocaine or crack during pregnancy can have devastating effects. Cocaine, which blocks the flow of blood to the fetus, has been found to cause a variety of structural defects (such as malformed limbs or damaged organs) and neurological problems. Babies of cocaine or crack addicts are also at risk for low birth weight, severe and persistent irritability, and learning disabilities.

A pregnant heroin addict has a higher than normal risk of complications during pregnancy and is more likely to have a premature or stillborn baby, or one who is low birth weight and small in size. Pregnant women on methadone face similar risks. The newborn baby of a mother addicted to heroin or methadone is also an addict at birth and must suffer through withdrawal.

Addictive drugs taken by a pregnant woman can cause her newborn baby to experience a long and painful period of withdrawal from the effects of the drugs. A baby going through withdrawal is likely to be extremely restless and irritable. He or she may scream incessantly, have difficulty sleeping, and fail to respond to efforts to provide comfort.

Use of an illegal recreational drug during pregnancy may cause problems in addition to those typically associated with the drug itself. Chemical contaminants and uncertain dosage, for example, are always a risk with drugs from street sources. In a few areas, law enforcement officials have attempted to prosecute women whose babies are born with evidence of maternal drug use.

If substance abuse is a problem for you, don't try to conceal it by avoiding prenatal care. The sooner you level with your caregiver, the sooner you and your baby can get the help you need and deserve.

During pregnancy, it's not just illegal drugs that may cause harm. An addictive substance such as Valium, even if it was prescribed for you under other circumstances, should not be taken while you are pregnant. (See also "Alcohol," page 78; "Marijuana," page 98; "Over-the-Counter Drugs," page 100; "Prescription Drugs and Medicines," page 104; and "Smoking," page 108.)

AEROBIC EXERCISE

A regular program of aerobic exercise during pregnancy can be beneficial, if you take care and use common sense. If you were fit prior to becoming pregnant, you probably can continue your regular workout routine as long as you feel up to it. Pregnancy is not, however, a time to undertake strenuous activity you've never tried before. Ask your caregiver if there are any special problems with your pregnancy that might make aerobic exercise inadvisable. Here are some general guidelines:

- Warm up gradually and cool down slowly.
- Avoid any exercise that raises your heart rate to more than 140 beats per minute or your body temperature to over 100.6°F. After the fourth month of pregnancy, don't do any exercise that requires you to lie on your back.
- High-impact aerobics may place too much strain on weight-bearing joints. Switch to a low-impact program. Your local pool may even have underwater aerobics classes. Water workouts are ideal for the pregnant body.
- Don't push too hard. If you're so out of breath that you can't talk and work out at the same time, you're overdoing it. Slow down.
- Wear comfortable clothing and appropriate athletic shoes. Wear a support bra while you exercise.

Ask your prenatal care provider about aerobics classes and other exercise programs that might be available for pregnant women in your community. If you want a structured program but prefer not to join a class, check your local library, bookstore, or video store for suitable exercise videos. *The American College of Obstetrics and Gynecology Pregnancy Exercise Program* is one video you might find helpful. Another video program developed especially for exercise during pregnancy is *Jane Fonda's New Pregnancy Workout.* (See also "Exercise," page 92; "Sports," page 108; and Section Three, "Keeping Healthy and Fit," pages 68–74.)

AIDS

AIDS (acquired immune deficiency syndrome) is a cluster of life-threatening ailments in individuals infected by the human immunodeficiency virus (HIV), which destroys the immune system of its victims.

HIV is a sexually transmitted disease that can be acquired through oral, vaginal, or anal intercourse when bodily fluids (such as blood, semen, vaginal secretions, or saliva) from an infected person enter the bloodstream of his or her partner. Infected needles or syringes also can transmit HIV, putting intravenous drug users at very high risk.

HIV is not thought to be contagious through casual contact; its transmission seems to require some exchange of bodily fluids. If either parent has AIDS or is a carrier of the disease (that is, is HIV-positive), however, a child born to those parents may be at risk. There is some evidence that the second pregnancy of a woman who is HIV positive or who actually has AIDS may be more dangerous than the first pregnancy, both for mother and for baby.

Although there is still much that we don't know about HIV and AIDS, ongoing research does provide some guidance and hope. Findings of a recent federal study, for example, indicate that treating an HIV-infected pregnant woman with the drug AZT may, in a significant number of cases, prevent her baby from contracting the disease. Recent research has found that rapid delivery (within four hours of the water breaking) reduces the likelihood of an infant becoming infected during the birth process, while infants born after prolonged labor seem to be at greater risk. Data on HIV-infected newborns suggest that about half contracted the disease in the womb, while the other half became infected during the birth process. The potential for special precautions to be used during delivery of HIV-positive mothers is a topic of continued study.

If you suspect that the AIDS virus might be a problem for you or your partner, there are positive steps you can take to protect your unborn child. Your prenatal care provider can give you the latest information, in confidence, on how to detect the disease and deal with it if necessary.

ALCOHOL

If you drink, you should keep in mind that the placenta does not keep alcohol away from your unborn child. Every time you take a drink, so does your baby.

Although in some cases the negative effect of alcohol on a developing baby may be temporary, research indicates that long-term, irreparable problems may be caused. Daily consumption of the amount of alcohol in two typical drinks (for example, two 1½-ounce shots of whiskey, two 5-ounce glasses of wine, or two 12-ounce cans of beer) has been associated with increased incidence of miscarriage and lower birth weight.

Children of heavy drinkers may be born with a condition known as fetal alcohol syndrome (FAS), the name given to an identifiable pattern of physical and mental difficulties. Babies with FAS may be smaller and less well formed than other babies, with physical problems such as kidney disorders, heart defects, genital malformations, or abnormal facial features. Fetal alcohol syndrome is the leading known cause of mental retardation in the United States. Many FAS babies are mentally retarded and/or neurologically impaired. Less severely affected infants may have lower birth weight, learning disabilities, and a tendency to be hyperactive or irritable.

The more often a woman drinks, and the larger the quantity of alcohol she consumes, the greater the risks. It is simply not known what amount of alcohol, if any, is safe for a pregnant woman and her unborn child. The surgeon general of the United States advises that pregnant women consume no alcohol whatsoever. In addition to avoiding beer, wine, and spirits, beware of hidden sources of alcohol, such as cough medicines and cold remedies.

We do not know how much drinking is too much, but we do know that it is not just the daily drinker who is at risk. An occasional crash binge in which great amounts are taken at one time may cause harm as well. It's best to save any celebrations involving alcohol until after your baby is born.

If you would like to stop drinking and are having trouble, don't be afraid to talk about it during a visit to your prenatal care provider. Asking for help is not a sign of weakness.

ALPHA FETOPROTEIN (AFP) TEST _____

Alpha fetoprotein (AFP) is a substance produced by the fetal liver. It crosses the placenta into the mother's bloodstream, where a routine blood test can measure it. A measure of AFP may be used for prenatal detection of neural tube defects (birth defects such as spina bifida or anencephaly). This screening is usually done by means of a blood sample taken between fifteen and twenty weeks of pregnancy. If the AFP level is outside the range known to be associated with normal development, the test should be repeated. If necessary, additional diagnostic procedures such as ultrasound (see page 112) or amniocentesis (see page 80) will be recommended.

While the cause of an abnormally high level of alpha fetoprotein may be a neural tube defect such as spina bifida (open spine) or anencephaly (absence of a brain), it may not be. High levels of AFP are also found in mothers carrying twins and sometimes in cases of threatened miscarriage. A very low level of AFP may indicate the possibility of Down syndrome.

If, because of other risk factors such as age or family history, a woman has already elected to have amniocentesis, the AFP level can be tested in the amniotic fluid. In such cases, the blood-screening test for alpha fetoprotein would not be necessary.

ALTERNATIVE BIRTH SETTINGS _____

To achieve a family-centered birthing experience in a homelike setting but without the potential hazards of home birth, many women are turning to alternative birth settings within or affiliated with a hospital.

In direct response to consumer demand, many hospitals now offer birthing rooms in which a woman may labor, deliver, recover, and bond with her newborn all in one place before moving to the regular maternity and nursery facilities. In some hospitals, birthing room facilities may be limited and available on a first come, first served basis. If such is the case, making your request known early may be helpful.

A number of hospitals have taken the birthing room concept one step further and established alternative birth centers separate from the regular obstetric units. These alternative centers, which offer maximum homelike flexibility and minimum intervention, may be limited to those women classified as "low risk."

Another option for low-risk women is a birth center outside the hospital. In these centers, most deliveries are handled by certified nurse-midwives. The emphasis is on dealing with birth as a normal process, but these birth centers have backup arrangements with nearby hospitals in case additional medical intervention is required.

Early in your pregnancy, you might wish to visit the various facilities available to you so that you can make an informed choice.

AMNIOCENTESIS _____

Amniocentesis is a diagnostic procedure that can be used to detect certain birth defects early in pregnancy and, later on, to assess the maturity of the fetus. Amniocentesis involves inserting a needle into the womb and removing a small amount of amniotic fluid. During the procedure, ultrasound is used to identify the precise location of the fetus and the placenta so that the examiner knows where to insert the needle. Laboratory examination of the fluid's cells (a process that may take two to three weeks) can detect the presence of a number of genetic defects.

Perhaps the most common use of amniocentesis is to detect the presence of Down syndrome in a woman who is over age thirty-five. The chances of bearing a child with Down syndrome, a chromosomal abnormality that causes mental retardation and physical malformation, increase sharply with the age of the mother. Amniocentesis can also detect neural tube defects and such diseases as sickle cell anemia and Tay-Sachs disease.

Amniocentesis to detect genetic defects is usually done during the 13th to 16th week of pregnancy. If a woman finds she is carrying a child with a particular genetic disorder, she might choose to terminate the pregnancy. For a woman at risk to find out that her child does *not* have the feared genetic defect would be reassuring. Ruling out certain disorders does not, however, guarantee a healthy baby. There are many birth defects that amniocentesis cannot detect.

Amniocentesis also may be used later in pregnancy to assess the health and development of the baby. For example, analysis of the amniotic fluid can determine the degree of fetal lung maturity. Such information could be of vital importance should there be reasons to contemplate delivery before term.

Amniocentesis is expensive, and it is not completely without risk to the fetus. In cases of advanced maternal age or certain family backgrounds, however, the benefits of the information obtained may outweigh the risks of the procedure. If you have questions about amniocentesis, you should discuss the pros and cons with your prenatal care provider to help you decide whether or not it is an appropriate procedure for your situation.

(See "Chorionic Villus Sampling (CVS)," page 85; "Down Syndrome," page 88; and "Genetic Counseling," page 93.)

AMNIOTOMY

Amniotomy is the artificial and intentional rupture of the membranes (breaking of the bag of waters) surrounding the baby. This procedure, which is done with a sterile instrument, does not cause pain for the mother. Artificial rupture of membranes is used to induce or to speed up labor, and to permit the insertion of an internal electronic fetal monitor.

Amniotomy is a very commonly used intervention. It is not, however, without its opponents. Those who object to its use point out that the amniotic sac does offer some protection to the baby's head during labor. If not broken artificially, the membranes are likely to rupture spontaneously by the end of the first stage of labor, although they may not. It is possible for a baby to be born with the bag of waters still intact.

Many women and their caregivers are comfortable with the routine use of amniotomy. Some, however, are not. If you have any questions about the use of this procedure in your case, ask your care provider. You may wish to request that amniotomy not be done routinely, but only if needed in the event of fetal distress.

AUTOMOBILE SAFETY

Being pregnant is not a reason to stop driving your car. You may continue to drive as long as you feel up to it and fit behind the wheel while still reaching the pedals. Do not sit in the vehicle for extended periods of time, either as a driver or as a passenger. Stop every hour or so and walk around for a few minutes to stimulate your circulation.

Whether or not you are pregnant, wearing a seat belt greatly reduces your risk of serious injury or death in an automobile accident. Fasten your seat belt so that the lap part of the belt is snug across your upper thighs and under your protruding abdomen and the shoulder strap is positioned between your breasts. Even if your vehicle has air bags, it's necessary to use the lap and shoulder belts for full protection.

If you are tempted to use your pregnancy as an excuse not to bother with seat belts, think again.

- The commonly held belief that seat belts may harm an unborn child has no basis in fact. A correctly positioned seat belt does not increase risk of fetal injury in a survivable crash.
- Don't worry about the shoulder strap damaging your breasts. Even if a breast is temporarily pressed by the strap, no serious harm is likely.
- Most automobile accidents occur within twenty-five miles of home. You and your unborn child need seat belts even on those short trips to the shopping mall or on your prenatal care visits.
- Death of the mother is a major cause of fetal death in a car crash. Using a seat belt can save your life and your baby's life along with it.

Before your baby is born, you should obtain an infant restraint system if you plan to transport your baby by car. Beginning with the trip home from the hospital, be sure to secure your child in an approved safety seat *every time* you travel in a motor vehicle.

BATHS

You may take regular tub baths or showers, whichever you prefer, throughout your pregnancy (unless your bag of waters has broken). Because recent research indicates that extremely high temperatures may harm a fetus, especially during early pregnancy, the temperature of your bath water should not exceed 100°F. You should avoid saunas, steam baths, and health club hot tubs as well as overheated home baths throughout pregnancy and especially during the first trimester. As your size and weight increase, be careful not to lose your balance getting in and out of the bathtub.

If your bag of waters has broken, do not take a tub bath. Take a shower instead. There is a danger of infection once the membranes have ruptured.

IMPORTANT: Keep your bath water 100°F or less.
Extremely hot temperatures can cause fetal damage.

BIOPHYSICAL PROFILE

The biophysical profile (BPP) is an indicator of fetal well-being based on an examination of the fetus using a combination of ultrasound and a nonstress test. The nonstress test records fetal heart rate. Ultrasound is used to examine and measure fetal breathing, fetal body movement, fetal muscle tone, and the amount of amniotic fluid. The placenta may be graded by development and/or age. Each item is scored, and then a total is obtained. The results of the BPP can help your care provider make decisions about your care and whether or not to induce labor. Especially near the end of a high-risk pregnancy, the BPP may be repeated as needed and the current score compared to previously recorded results to aid in decision making.

BONDING _____

Bonding is the development of attachment between two individuals. Bonding between mother and baby, between father and baby, or between baby and siblings or other family members is a process, not something that happens or fails to happen in an instant. For mother and baby, the bonding process has begun long before birth. The baby, who can hear while in the womb, knows the mother's voice and instinctively turns to it after birth. A newborn may also recognize the father's voice or others heard regularly before being born.

The time immediately after delivery is valuable for the bonding process. This is a time when mother, father, and baby can establish and enjoy closeness as a family. Newborns are far more aware of what is going on around them than once thought. Not only can a newborn recognize and respond to familiar voices, but he or she can distinguish shapes up to a foot away, thus making early eye contact with the parents possible.

Skin contact between parents and baby provides warmth and security. If possible, the newborn should be placed on the mother's abdomen, prior to being clothed or wrapped, immediately after birth. If the mother plans to breastfeed, the baby should be put to the breast as soon as possible.

How can you prepare for bonding? Discuss with your caregiver your wishes for some quiet time free of medical interventions right after your baby is born. Staff in some birth settings not only allow but also encourage practices that facilitate bonding right from the start. Use of medication in the baby's eyes to prevent infection may, for example, be delayed an hour or more to enable parents and baby to enjoy eye contact. Measuring, weighing, washing, wrapping, or administering other procedures in the hospital routine usually can wait awhile. How important this is to you may influence your choice of birth setting. It's important to discuss your preferences with your prenatal caregiver in advance.

Although the time immediately after your baby's birth can be very special, all is not lost if things do not work out as planned. If, for example, a medical emergency prevents you and your baby from sharing the earliest moments after delivery, it's important to remember that the bonding process can successfully resume as soon as you both are able.

BREASTFEEDING PREPARATION _____

If you plan to breastfeed your baby, you may wish to try one or more of the following during pregnancy. These measures may help prevent nipple soreness when you first start to feed your baby.

- Rub your nipples gently with a terry cloth towel at least twice a day.
- Use water with little or no soap for washing your nipples.
- Hold each nipple between your fingers and gently pull and roll it for a minute, twice daily. You may use cream or oil if you wish.
- Go without a bra, or wear a nursing bra with the flaps down for some time each day. This exposes your nipples to air and to the gentle friction of your clothing.

If you have flat or inverted (turning inward) nipples, there is a special breast shield you can wear to help extend the nipples and draw them out. Ask your prenatal caregiver if you need help.

An excellent source of assistance for mothers who wish to breastfeed is La Leche League International, 9616 Minneapolis Avenue, Franklin Park, Ill. 60131. Its phone number is (708) 445-7730. Its toll-free number, (800) LA LECHE, is staffed part time, and a recording will direct you to emergency assistance should you need it at any other time. Your prenatal caregiver may be able to direct you to La Leche League volunteers in your area.

BREECH PRESENTATION

More than 95 percent of the babies delivered present themselves in a headfirst position. Occasionally, however, the baby is turned so that the buttocks or another body part is closest to the cervix. This is called a breech presentation. Sometimes a baby in a breech position will turn naturally before the mother goes into labor. Sometimes the birth attendant will be able to turn the baby prior to delivery. Although it is possible for a baby to be born other than head first, many breech presentations require a Caesarean section. Your prenatal care provider will discuss this with you should it be necessary. If you have questions or concerns, be sure to ask.

CAESAREAN DELIVERY

You should keep in mind that a Caesarean (also spelled cesarean) delivery is always a possibility, although for many women that possibility is a small one. In some situations, such as small pelvic opening and large baby or certain breech presentations, the need for a Caesarean can be predicted in advance. If this is true in your case, you would have a chance to prepare for it and ask any questions you might have in advance. In other circumstances—fetal distress, for example—the decision for a Caesarean would be made on the spot by your birth attendant during your labor.

In a Caesarean delivery, a surgical incision is made in the mother's abdomen and uterus in order to remove the baby. In preparation for a Caesarean, a small amount of blood may be drawn from the mother for analysis, her pubic area and abdomen may be shaved, and she will be given an IV and a urinary catheter. Regional anesthesia such as an epidural (see page 91) or spinal has a number of advantages, although certain circumstances, such as a need to move very rapidly, may necessitate general anesthesia. Use of regional anesthesia enables the mother to remain conscious and aware during delivery, and it tends to pose fewer risks.

Caesarean deliveries generally work out well for both mother and baby, although the recovery time may be slightly longer for the mother than it would have been for a vaginal delivery. A Caesarean mother can breastfeed her baby, although for a day or two she may need help placing the baby in a comfortable position.

If you should require a Caesarean delivery, many hospitals will allow your partner to stay with you for the birth if the two of you are comfortable with the idea. If you know that remaining together at such a time would be very important to you, it's best to discuss this with your prenatal care provider in advance to make sure your wishes will be accommodated. If you have any questions about the possible need for a Caesarean in your case, you should ask. In the event that a Caesarean is required, feel free to ask about any of the procedures as they occur.

It was once thought that a woman who delivered one baby by Caesarean section would be required to have any future children in the same way. This is no longer correct. Depending on the reason for the previous Caesarean and your present condition, delivery of your baby vaginally may be not only possible, but also preferable to another Caesarean. Discuss this with your caregiver well in advance of your due date. (See Vaginal Birth After Caesarean, page 113.)

If you are concerned about Caesarean delivery, an excellent source of information and encouragement is the International Cesarean Awareness Network, P.O. Box 152, Syracuse, N.Y. 13210. You can write to the organization at that address or call (315) 424-1942.

CHLAMYDIA _____

Chlamydia is at present the most common sexually transmitted disease in the United States. Chlamydia can infect the urethra, anus, or pelvic organs of a woman and is a cause of pelvic inflammatory disease. Chlamydia also can cause eye infections. Painful intercourse, burning, frequent urination, and abdominal pain may all be symptoms of chlamydia. As many as three-fourths of the women with chlamydia infections, however, may experience no symptoms at all.

Many prenatal care providers now test routinely for chlamydia. Even if she has no symptoms, a pregnant woman with chlamydia can transmit the infection to her baby during delivery. An infant who contracts chlamydia in the birth canal may develop pneumonia or infections of the eyes, ears, nose, throat, or digestive system.

If you have chlamydia, it's important to receive treatment so that you won't communicate the infection to your baby during delivery. Tetracycline, typically the treatment of choice for the nonpregnant woman with chlamydia, should not be used during pregnancy. Your care provider will prescribe a medication such as erythromycin, which is safer for you at this time. Unless your partner is treated as well, you are likely to be reinfected. Use of a condom during intercourse may also help reduce the risk of reinfection.

CHORIONIC VILLUS SAMPLING (CVS) _____

Chorionic villus sampling (CVS) is a procedure that analyzes samples of placental tissue to assess fetal well-being. Some medical centers offer CVS as an alternative to amniocentesis. The technique can be used at eight to twelve weeks of pregnancy, with the results obtained about two weeks after that. A preliminary analysis that would indicate the presence of Down syndrome can be done within forty-eight hours.

In a scenario where a woman would consider pregnancy termination as an option, the earlier availability of information would be an advantage. Disadvantages of CVS include a somewhat higher rate of failure to obtain information and a slightly higher rate of spontaneous abortion (miscarriage) following the procedure. Another disadvantage is that CVS, unlike amniocentesis, does not test for alpha fetoprotein (see page 79). If the alpha fetoprotein test reveals a high level of protein, amniocentesis may still be recommended for a more complete diagnostic picture (see page 80).

CONTRACTION STRESS TEST

The contraction stress test may be used in a high-risk late pregnancy as one of the measures to evaluate placental functioning and fetal well-being. In a contraction stress test (often referred to as the oxytocin challenge test, or OCT), contractions of the uterus are induced and a fetal heart monitor is used to record the responses of the fetus to these contractions. To stimulate contractions in a stress test, the drug oxytocin may be administered intravenously in a low dose. An alternate method of inducing contractions for the test involves having the woman massage one or both of her nipples. The contractions brought on in this way are mild and relatively painless. They rarely persist for more than an hour or so after the stimulation is withdrawn.

A contraction stress test may be used in suspected cases of postmaturity (overdue baby) or to assist in decision making when there are risk factors such as diabetes, preeclampsia (toxemia), hypertension, or a small-for-dates baby. The results of the stress test may indicate that the pregnancy should be permitted to continue longer. If not, the results will help the caregiver decide whether to induce labor or perform a Caesarean section.

DENTAL CARE

It's a good idea to visit your dentist early in your pregnancy and have a thorough professional cleaning of your teeth and gums. During pregnancy, your mouth's normal bacteria and acid-alkaline balance may change and make you more prone to cavities. Many women experience tenderness and inflammation of the gums during pregnancy, making a personal program of oral hygiene especially necessary. Don't be tempted to let temporary discomfort of tender gums interfere with daily brushing and flossing (see "Gums [Bleeding and Swelling]," page 26).

Be sure to inform your dentist that you are pregnant. If you have mitral valve prolapse or a similar condition that requires the use of prophylactic antibiotics prior to undergoing dental procedures, you must take an antibiotic that is safe for you and your baby during pregnancy. Ask your prenatal care provider about this. He or she may wish to contact the dentist directly.

Avoid X rays during the first four months of your pregnancy. If absolutely necessary later in your pregnancy, dental X rays may be done using a protective shield. If possible, however, it's better to postpone treatment that requires X rays until after your baby is born.

DIABETES

Diabetes is a disease in which there is an imbalance between sugar in the body and the body's insulin supply. This imbalance and its effects may intensify during pregnancy, with serious consequences for both mother and fetus. Before the availability of synthetic insulin, the pregnancy of a diabetic woman had little chance of a successful outcome. Now, however, careful medical monitoring can help a diabetic woman increase her chances of having a healthy baby.

A diabetic pregnancy is a high-risk one. Diabetics are more likely to develop pre-eclampsia (toxemia), have stillbirths during the last two weeks or so of term, or have abnormally large babies. For these reasons, delivery by Caesarean section before term is sometimes indicated.

If you are diabetic, it's especially important that you follow recommendations regarding diet and medication and that you see your physician for regular checkups. It's best if your prenatal caregiver works directly with your regular doctor. Your prenatal appointments will be scheduled on a more frequent basis than they would be for most pregnant women. The insulin requirements for a diabetic woman will change as pregnancy progresses. Frequent (several times a day) self-testing for blood sugar may be required, along with a daily test of urine for ketone bodies.

(See "Gestational Diabetes," page 94.)

DISABILITY BENEFITS

Although pregnancy itself is not an illness, the law requires that pregnancy-related conditions be treated in the same way as other temporary disabilities or illness for purposes of sick leave or disability insurance. If you are employed during pregnancy, you may be entitled to certain sick leave and/or disability benefits from your employer.

If you are unable to work because of your pregnancy, you should check with your employer to see what benefits, if any, are provided. Find out if the requirements of the recently enacted federal family leave legislation apply to your employer. If so, your employer can tell you how the provisions of the law affect your options during pregnancy. Your local unemployment office can advise you about the availability of unemployment or temporary disability benefits in your state. Don't be afraid to discuss these matters with your prenatal care provider. Chances are, the office staff has filled out all of the required forms many times before.

DIURETICS

Years ago, diuretics ("water pills") were routinely prescribed to help a pregnant woman reduce the swelling (edema) in her legs caused by fluid retention. This type of medication, however, flushes out needed substances along with the unwanted fluids, and continued use may harm the baby. Diuretics, therefore, are no longer recommended during pregnancy for treatment of edema.

Never take a diuretic on your own while you are pregnant. (See page 33 for alternative ways of dealing with the problem of fluid retention during pregnancy.)

DOUCHING

Do not douche during pregnancy unless your prenatal caregiver explicitly orders it for a medical reason and explains how to go about it. Douching during pregnancy can be dangerous. If you have a vaginal infection, douching incorrectly could introduce the infection to your uterus. While pregnant, unlike any other time, it is possible to introduce air into your circulatory system under pressure from the douche solution. This could cause serious complications, even death. In late pregnancy, douching could cause your bag of waters to break.

If vaginal discomfort, itching, or unpleasant odor are bothersome, report the condition to your health-care provider. Don't be tempted to self-medicate using an over-the-counter douche preparation. In addition to the general risks associated with douching during pregnancy, some commercial douche products contain iodine or other ingredients with the potential to harm the fetus.

(See "Vaginal Discharge," page 35.)

DOWN SYNDROME

Down syndrome (or Down's syndrome) is a chromosomal abnormality that causes mental retardation and physical malformation. Down syndrome (also known as Trisomy 21, because it is caused by the presence of an extra copy of the 21st chromosome) occurs in about 1 in 750 births overall, but the chances of having a child with this condition increase sharply with the age of the mother. At age thirty-five, for example, the chances of a woman having a baby with Down syndrome are about 1 in 365, while at age forty-five the risk rises to about 1 in 40.

The option of amniocentesis (see page 80), which can detect such birth defects as Down syndrome, is routinely offered to women over age thirty-five. In some medical centers, chorionic villus sampling (see page 85) is available as an alternative to amniocentesis. If a woman would be unwilling to terminate a pregnancy under any circumstances, whether or not to have such tests should be carefully considered. (See also "Genetic Counseling," page 93.)

ECTOPIC PREGNANCY

In a routine pregnancy, the fertilized ovum moves down the fallopian tube into the uterus, where it implants and develops. In a small percentage of cases, however, something goes wrong and the pregnancy develops in the tube or, in extremely rare instances, in the abdominal or pelvic area outside the womb. This is called an ectopic ("out of place") pregnancy. Failure to identify and remove an ectopic pregnancy can result in hemorrhage and even death for the mother.

Although it's possible for a woman with no known risk factors to have an ectopic pregnancy, such a condition is more likely in women with tubal abnormalities. Women who have had pelvic inflammatory disease, endometriosis, fertility problems, abdominal surgery, or a previous ectopic pregnancy are at higher risk for tubal abnormalities. A woman whose pregnancy resulted from a contraceptive failure involving an intrauterine device (IUD), unsuccessful tubal sterilization, or contraceptive implant is also at risk for an ectopic pregnancy.

Signs of an ectopic pregnancy may include any or all of the following:

- Dull or sharp abdominal pain that may come on suddenly and persist or, in other cases, ache somewhat intermittently;
- Erratic vaginal bleeding, either lighter or heavier than typical menstrual bleeding;
- Weakness, dizziness or fainting, or headaches;
- Shoulder pain (caused by excessive blood in the abdomen resulting from a ruptured tube).

If you experience any of these symptoms, consult your prenatal care provider without delay. If an ectopic pregnancy is suspected, one or more tests will be done to confirm or rule out that diagnosis. A blood test for the hormone human chorionic gonadotropin (HCG), which increases as a pregnancy progresses, may indicate an abnormal increase of this hormone, a situation that is more likely to occur in an ectopic pregnancy. Abnormal results of a test for the hormone progesterone also may indicate a possible ectopic pregnancy, although similar results may be found in cases of threatened miscarriage as well.

Although tubal pregnancy is difficult to see with ultrasound, an ultrasound exam that finds a pregnancy in the uterus would indicate that ectopic pregnancy is unlikely. Transvaginal ultrasound, a newer technique than the traditional sonogram, may provide a better picture in early pregnancy. (See "Ultrasound," page 112.)

Laparoscopy is a test in which a device is inserted through a small incision in the abdomen. The instrument, which magnifies and illuminates, enables the physician to see the fallopian tubes. A small ectopic pregnancy that has not ruptured the tube sometimes can be removed during a laparoscopy. If the pregnancy is large or the tube has already ruptured, more extensive surgery will be required. A ruptured tube is an emergency and must be handled without delay.

In a few cases, drugs to halt the growth of the pregnancy and allow the body to reabsorb the tissue may be feasible. This relatively new treatment can be used only if the ectopic pregnancy has been detected early enough to be very small, without rupture of the tube and without bleeding. This treatment is not yet available at some hospitals.

Early treatment of an ectopic pregnancy is essential not only for a woman's own health but also for her future reproductive capacity. Don't hesitate to call your prenatal caregiver if there is any hint that you might have a problem. It's better to find out that nothing is wrong than to risk waiting until a treatable condition becomes a life-threatening emergency.

ELECTRONIC FETAL MONITORING

Electronic fetal monitoring is a means of continuously observing the baby's heartbeat to check his or her condition in the womb during labor. There are two types of electronic monitoring: internal and external. The internal monitor uses an electrode attached to the baby's scalp to record fetal heart rate. An electrode placed inside the mother's uterus records contractions. Unless the membranes have ruptured spontaneously, an amniotomy must be performed before an internal monitor can be used. The external monitor, which is less accurate than the internal type, is strapped around the mother's abdomen and uses ultrasound to record fetal heart rate and a pressure sensor to record contractions.

Monitoring by a nurse or other birth attendant using a hand-held, ultrasonic stethoscope is an alternative. With a one-nurse-per-laboring-woman ratio, monitoring by a trained person can be as reliable and safe for the baby as continuous electronic monitoring. Some women prefer not to be attached to a device that limits their freedom to assume any comfortable position and move around the room freely during labor. Others, however, feel more secure when connected to a high-tech device for continuous monitoring.

Some hospitals and caregivers use electronic fetal monitoring routinely. Others employ the devices only when specifically indicated for high-risk deliveries. Routine use of electronic monitoring has been associated with an increase in the chances of Caesarean delivery. You may wish to discuss with your caregiver in advance whether or not electronic fetal monitoring will be recommended or required in your situation. Feel free to ask any questions you might have.

EMPLOYMENT

Depending on your health and the nature of your job, you probably can continue to work as long as you wish. In the past, some employers discriminated against women who became pregnant and set arbitrary limits on the length of time a pregnant woman could continue on the job. Such an attitude, however, is no longer legally permitted; nor is it medically recommended. Many women choose to work throughout pregnancy. If you and your baby are healthy and the nature of your job does not pose insurmountable dangers to your pregnancy, how long you work should be up to you.

If you suspect that the nature of your job may place you or your baby at risk, discuss this with your prenatal caregiver early in your pregnancy. (See "Workplace Hazards," pages 115–6, for a more detailed discussion of the types of employment that may be dangerous during pregnancy.) Your employer may have specific information relevant to potential problems in your specific job category. Your state or local health department may be another source of information on job-related hazards during pregnancy.

You probably can continue to do the tasks you did before you were pregnant as long as you feel up to it. If there is some special problem with your pregnancy that would require you to modify your activities, your caregiver will discuss this with you.

If your job is physically strenuous, the normal fatigue of pregnancy is likely to affect you no matter how fit you may be. As your size and shape change, you will have to be careful doing things in which balance is involved. If your job requires you to sit, it's important to get up and walk around for a few minutes every hour or two. This will help prevent circulation slowdown and clot formation. If your job requires you to stand for long periods, try to schedule breaks during which you can rest with your feet up for a few minutes. Use common sense, and listen to your body.

(See also "Disability Benefits," page 87.)

ENEMA

In a few hospitals, ordering an enema for a laboring woman may still be a typical procedure following admission, but most birth attendants now consider routine enemas to be unnecessary. The purpose of the enema is to empty the lower bowel to give the baby more room as well as to minimize the involuntary expulsion of stool during labor. For many women, however, nature provides its own cleansing process, and bowel movements or diarrhea empty the bowels naturally before or during early labor.

You should be able to choose not to have an enema. You may wish to discuss this matter with your caregiver in advance.

EPIDURAL ANESTHESIA

A woman who has a Caesarean delivery will, of course, require anesthesia. Although general anesthesia, which can be administered rapidly, may be used in an emergency, a regional anesthetic such as an epidural is preferred in most situations.

An epidural is administered through a slender tube that is inserted by needle between two vertebrae in the lower back. The tube is taped in place to permit infusion of the anesthetic continuously or intermittently into the epidural canal as needed. An epidural leaves the woman fully conscious but numbs the pain nerves from the waist down. It is safe for the baby.

If you have an epidural for a Caesarean, some hospitals may require your partner to leave while it is administered. If you feel strongly about being together the entire time, this may be a negotiable item.

Epidural anesthesia also can be used for pain relief in a vaginal birth. If total absence of pain is very important to you, you may wish to consider it. There are, however, a number of drawbacks. Although you would be conscious, your ability to push in the second stage of labor would be reduced. There would be an increased chance that forceps or a vacuum extractor would be necessary to deliver your baby. In some cases, the failure to progress caused in part by the effects of an epidural might even lead to a decision to perform a Caesarean section.

While it would be nice if the pain relief afforded by an epidural could be achieved without affecting other aspects of the birthing experience, it doesn't usually work that way. If you opt for an epidural for pain relief during labor, you invite other inevitable interventions. A medical specialist from a different discipline—anesthesiology—would join your caregiver and become an integral part of what goes on during your labor.

With an epidural, you probably would be required to have an intravenous drip, an internal fetal monitor (and an amniotomy if your membranes haven't ruptured spontaneously), an external monitor to record contractions, and perhaps a cardiac monitor for yourself as well. Although an epidural may leave you with motor function even as it numbs the pain, you wouldn't be able to walk around with all those devices attached even if you wanted to.

If you are thinking of having an epidural for a vaginal delivery, it's important that your decision be a fully informed one. For some women, the trade-off is worth it. For many, it is not.

EPISIOTOMY

An episiotomy is an incision in the perineum (the area between the vagina and anus) to enlarge the birth opening. The purpose of an episiotomy is to keep the perineum from tearing and to hasten delivery.

If you have an episiotomy, it will be done just before the baby's head is delivered. A local anesthetic such as novocaine will be used unless you already have had a general or regional anesthetic. After the baby is born and the placenta delivered, the incision will be stitched. (See page 144 for suggestions on how to ease the discomfort from an episiotomy as the incision heals.)

Some birth attendants do episiotomies routinely. Others evaluate the need for one on a case-by-case basis. If you feel strongly that you would prefer to avoid an episiotomy if at all possible, be sure to communicate your wishes in advance to your prenatal care provider. You may wish to discuss with your caregiver in advance whether or not an episiotomy might be necessary in your situation. No matter what your preference, however, it's possible that an episiotomy may turn out to be necessary to prevent severe tearing or to hasten delivery for the baby's sake.

You can help increase your chance of delivery without an episiotomy or tearing by doing the Kegel exercises described on pages 68–9. These exercises, if done regularly, will prepare and strengthen your perineum for delivery.

EXERCISE

A regular program of exercise will enhance your physical condition and comfort not only during pregnancy but also during labor, delivery, and afterward. If you are fit and your body feels good, you will be happier and more confident. Women who are active during pregnancy tend to have fewer health problems, less fatigue, and a quicker return to full activity after delivery.

When you exercise, common sense and the way you feel should be your guide. As your weight and center of gravity change, it's especially important to work with rather than against your body. Don't exercise to the point of pain or exhaustion, and don't engage in an activity that causes overheating or raises your heart rate to more than 140 beats per minute. Be sure to warm up gradually to more strenuous routines and allow adequate time to cool down between activities. After the fourth month of pregnancy, avoid exercises that involve lying flat on the back, because pressure from your heavy uterus on a major blood vessel can diminish blood flow to your heart and to the placenta.

Swimming or walking will benefit your entire body and are especially good sources of exercise during pregnancy. A brisk daily walk may help prevent circulatory problems. (See "Aerobic Exercise," page 77, and "Sports," page 108, for additional information to help you choose suitable activities.)

The pelvic floor (Kegel) exercises beginning on page 68 and the exercises for abdominal muscles on pages 72–3 are designed to help you strengthen muscles you will need in labor and delivery. You will find these exercises useful after your baby is born as well as during pregnancy.

FORCEPS DELIVERY

Forceps, which look somewhat like salad tongs, are sometimes used to help pull the baby through the birth canal if the second stage of labor is not progressing and the mother is unable to push the baby out. Although forceps have been associated with increased risk of birth injury, they can be safely employed by a skilled birth attendant experienced in their use. A low-forceps delivery involves using the instrument when the baby's head is at the perineum. A midforceps delivery, which is more difficult, involves using the instrument when the baby's head is not yet at the perineum but is still in the midportion of the pelvis. Although certain caregivers will use a midforceps delivery with confidence, others prefer to perform a Caesarean in similar circumstances. The physician's skill and experience with each technique will influence the decision about which one to use. Use of forceps requires that the mother have anesthesia and an episiotomy.

Forceps deliveries occur less frequently now than they did in the past. In part this is due to emphasis on natural childbirth and the decrease in use of anesthesia (which impairs the ability to push) for vaginal deliveries. Use of birthing positions in which gravity is an aid (squatting, standing, sitting, or kneeling) may also reduce the need for forceps.

A vacuum extractor may be used instead of forceps. A vacuum cup is attached to the baby's head by suction, and the baby is drawn through the birth canal. Vacuum extraction has long been widely used in Europe, and its use as an alternative to forceps is increasing in the United States.

GENETIC COUNSELING

Couples concerned that they may be at above-average risk for having a child with an inherited disorder or birth defect may wish to consider genetic counseling as part of their decision-making process. Counseling by a trained professional can assist you in gathering and interpreting pertinent information in light of potential risks and available options. A genetic counselor will advise you on suitable diagnostic procedures—amniocentesis, for example (see page 80).

People in the following circumstances might find genetic counseling appropriate:

- Those who themselves have a birth defect or inherited disorder or who already have a child with such a problem
- Women over the age of thirty-five
- Women with a history of unexplained infant death or multiple miscarriages
- Those whose ethnic group places them at risk for certain genetic defects (for example, blacks for sickle cell anemia and Eastern European Jews for Tay-Sachs disease)
- Those concerned about exposure to personal and environmental hazards such as radiation, known carcinogens, chemicals, infections, medications, recreational and illegal drugs, chemotherapy, or any other potentially harmful substance.

A genetic counselor does not make decisions for you, but he or she can help you develop a sound basis for making your own decisions based on relevant facts within the framework of your personal value system and beliefs.

Your prenatal care provider should be able to suggest appropriate resources if genetic counseling is indicated in your case. Information also may be obtained from the National Center for Education in Maternal and Child Health, 3520 Prospect Street NW, Washington, D.C. 20057.

GENITAL HERPES

During its active stage, herpes virus (type 2) causes painful sores on the genitals. These sores or blisters may affect the vagina and cervix as well as the labia and rectum. There is no known cure, although a care provider may prescribe a medicated lotion to relieve the pain and to minimize the time the active lesions are contagious.

A pregnant woman who carries the herpes virus may be more likely to miscarry, give birth prematurely, or have a low birth weight baby. Careful medical management of pregnancy and delivery for a woman with herpes is especially important to help minimize the potential risks to the baby. If a woman has an active case of genital herpes at the time of delivery, the baby has a one in two chance of acquiring the disease in the birth canal. A newborn who has contracted herpes in this way may die or be severely handicapped with brain damage or blindness. Consequently, as the baby approaches term, delivery by Caesarean section is indicated for a mother with an active case of genital herpes.

To help prevent the spread of herpes, avoid oral sex if you or your partner have cold sores or fever blisters. The sores contain the active herpes virus, and you should wash your hands carefully before any genital contact. It is possible for oral herpes (type 1), which causes sores around the mouth, to cause sores on the genitals as well. If you or your partner have active genital herpes, use of a condom or abstinence from sexual activity involving genital contact is recommended.

(See "Sexually Transmitted Diseases," pages 106–7).

GESTATIONAL DIABETES

A small number of women (about 2 to 4 percent) develop diabetes during pregnancy even though they have no previous history of the disease. This condition, called gestational diabetes, is directly related to hormonal changes during pregnancy. It disappears after delivery.

Gestational diabetes usually doesn't appear until the third trimester of pregnancy or perhaps late in the second. A woman with gestational diabetes faces risks similar to those faced by women who are diabetic prior to pregnancy, although management of the condition may be somewhat less difficult in some cases.

It is usually possible to treat gestational diabetes with modifications to the diet and exercise. If the blood sugar level is extremely high or such measures are not successful, use of insulin may be required. If you develop gestational diabetes, you will have to work especially closely with your prenatal health-care team to monitor your condition and take whatever dietary and other measures may be needed. It may be necessary for you to self-test your blood sugar level frequently, perhaps several times a day. You will also require frequent urine tests. Fortunately, with good medical care and diligent efforts on your part, the chances for a successful outcome of your pregnancy are excellent.

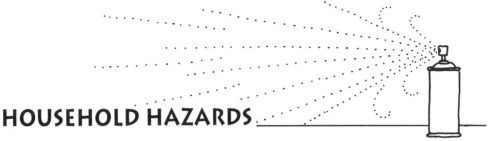

HOUSEHOLD HAZARDS

Most people think of home as a safe place to be. There are some common household hazards, however, that may make home not so safe and that may affect your pregnancy. Toxic substances, for example, should be avoided as much as possible at all times, especially during pregnancy. Cleaning substances, insecticides, pesticides, or any household or personal item in an aerosol spray can should be used with care, if at all. (See "Toxic Substances," pages 109–10.)

It's important to make certain that your home's tap water is safe to drink. If you get your water from a private well, make sure it is not contaminated. If your home has lead pipes or even copper pipes with lead solder, your drinking water may contain unacceptable concentrations of lead. You may wish to have it tested. If you obtain your water from a municipal water source, ask your local officials for data about its safety. You are entitled to this information. If you have questions about your municipal water supply, you can call the Environmental Protection Agency's (EPA's) Safe Drinking Water Hotline at (800) 426-4791 for information about federal standards for drinking water. Request the publications *Lead in Your Drinking Water* and *Is Your Drinking Water Safe?*

Lead is especially hazardous to young children and fetuses. If the pipes in your home are contributing to lead concentrations in your drinking water, you can reduce the amount of lead in the water by running the tap for approximately five minutes before using any of it for drinking or cooking. In other words, don't consume water that has been standing in the pipes for any period of time. (You don't have to waste it. Use it for cleaning or watering the plants.) Take water for drinking or cooking only from the cold water tap. Hot water is likely to have more lead because higher temperatures promote leaching. If you decide to use bottled water as an alternative, don't assume it's better than tap water. In fact, it may simply be more expensive. Ask the water supplier for data to help you make an informed decision.

Beware of hidden sources of lead in addition to what you might find in your water supply. Avoid peeling paint left over from the days when lead paints were legal. Colored glossy newspaper inserts and magazines or metallic giftwrap inks may have high lead content. Handle these items minimally, and don't burn them in your home fireplace. Don't use foreign-made pottery for food or beverages (unless it's been tested and proved safe), because the ceramic glaze may contain dangerously high levels of lead. Elegant as fine crystal may appear, don't store beverages in crystal decanters or drink from lead crystal glasses. Recent research has found that some of the lead may leave the crystal and end up in your drink.

During pregnancy (and at any other time), be careful of common household appliances that create electromagnetic fields. The extent to which these are hazardous is still a controversial issue. There is some indication, however, that chronic exposure to electromagnetic fields may be associated with reproductive problems and with childhood and adult cancers. It would be wise, therefore, to minimize exposure if you can.

Here are some suggestions for reducing exposure to electromagnetic fields.

- If you use a microwave, don't stand near it while it is operating.
- Let your hair dry naturally in preference to using an electric hair dryer. If you must use a dryer, keep it on the lowest setting and hold it as far away as you can and still get the job done.
- Sit six feet or more from your television, and turn it off when you're not watching it.
- If you use a home computer, keep at least two feet away from the monitor. Turn it off when you're not using it.
- Use a hot water bottle in preference to an electric heating pad. Avoid electric blankets and waterbeds with electric heaters. If you must use an electric blanket, make sure yours is a new model (manufactured since 1990) redesigned to reduce the problem of an electromagnetic field.

Beware of indoor air pollution in your home. Air fresheners, aerosol sprays, cleaning materials, artificial fireplace logs, paints, and solvents can all release chemicals with potentially harmful effects. Cigarette smoking by anyone in your home is a hazard to you and your unborn child. Ironically, if your house is well weatherproofed and energy efficient, you may have even more concerns than if you were able to open the windows and let in some fresh air.

If you use gas appliances for drying, cooking, or heating, have them checked for gas leaks. Make sure they are properly cleaned and vented to avoid buildup of carbon monoxide in your home. You can't see, smell, or taste carbon monoxide, but it can kill you. Kerosene space heaters are an especially dangerous source of indoor air pollution.

Outdoor air pollution may cause problems too. Where there is heavy automobile traffic, there is likely to be a high concentration of carbon monoxide. Avoid bumper-to-bumper traffic, tunnels, and indoor parking garages as much as possible. Let someone else walk behind the power lawn mower or leaf blower.

The potential problems posed by environmental pollution affect everyone, not just pregnant women and their unborn babies. Because the fetus is especially vulnerable, however, this is a good time for you to become informed and to take sensible steps to protect yourself and your entire family.

INDUCED LABOR

Labor can be started by the artificial rupture of membranes or by using the synthetic hormone oxytocin, which is given intravenously. Some care providers now offer the use of a prostaglandin gel applied vaginally to soften the cervix and induce contractions.

In the past, babies born "by appointment" were not uncommon because some physicians routinely induced labor and mothers often requested it. This practice, however, is now known to contain potential hazards for mother and baby and is not generally recommended.

There may be medical reasons to induce labor. These reasons include illness of the mother, such as preeclampsia or diabetes, or deterioration of placental functioning. In such circumstances, onset of labor is necessary for the health of the mother, the baby, or both. Convenience—yours or the caregiver's—is not a medical reason for induction. So even if you feel sure you have been pregnant too long, in most cases it's best to let nature take its course. If an induced labor is suggested for you, feel free to ask about the reasons.

KICK COUNT

In late pregnancy, you can monitor fetal movement without any special equipment by simply keeping a kick count. All you have to do is record the number of times your baby moves over a specific period of time. Your care provider will tell you when and how to do this sort of record keeping and what results to look for.

A variation of the kick count is the count-to-ten test. Instead of keeping track of every movement within a specific time period, you would begin at the same time each day and count each movement you feel until you have counted ten of them. Record the time you felt the tenth movement. If it is taking longer and longer as the days go by to reach the tenth movement, other tests may be suggested to assess fetal well-being. Your care provider will explain what to look for and what the results of your own monitoring of fetal movement might mean.

If you do not feel any fetal movement within a twelve-hour time period, tell your prenatal care provider without delay. Depending on the particular circumstances of your situation, your caregiver might tell you to call sooner, perhaps after six or eight hours, for example.

LEBOYER DELIVERY

The Leboyer method of delivery is described in detail by French obstetrician Frederick Leboyer in his book *Birth Without Violence* (see page 117). This approach to delivery is an effort to minimize trauma to the newborn by providing a gentle, loving atmosphere for birth. Leboyer's recommendations include a quiet and dimly lit environment, the immediate placement of the newborn on the mother's abdomen, waiting to cut the cord until it has stopped pulsating, and giving the baby a warm bath to ease the transition from the womb to the outside world. If this type of approach to delivery appeals to you, read Leboyer's book and discuss your wishes with your care provider. Some hospitals resist efforts to dim the lights and impose gentle ways in place of certain medical routines. If you believe a Leboyer style of gentle birth is important to your family, this may influence your choice of birth setting.

LOVEMAKING

Unless there is a special problem with your pregnancy, which your prenatal caregiver will discuss with you, you may make love throughout your nine months of pregnancy. No harm will come to you or your baby.

Vaginal bleeding, pain, or leakage of amniotic fluid are indications that intercourse may be inadvisable, and you should report any of these problems to your health-care team. Late in pregnancy, as your cervix begins to dilate, you may wish to use a condom as an extra precaution against infection.

Oral sex during pregnancy is permissible if you enjoy it, but we caution you and your partner not to allow air to be blown into your vagina. Because of the way your circulatory system changes to accommodate your pregnancy, it is possible for air bubbles (emboli) to enter the bloodstream at this time and cause serious damage, even death.

For some people, sexual desire is enhanced during pregnancy. For others, it is diminished. As your shape changes, you may be more comfortable with different positions or techniques. Don't be afraid to experiment. Talking together about your feelings at this time will help both you and your partner.

LYME DISEASE

Lyme disease is carried by deer ticks, which will attach to and feed on any handy host, including an available human. Infected ticks have been found in lawns and gardens as well as in fields and woods, so staying close to the house is no guarantee of safety.

Although a pregnant woman who contracts Lyme disease may have a healthy baby, severe or even fatal damage to an unborn child is possible. The disease can be treated with antibiotics, but prevention is preferable. When outdoors in an area that could harbor ticks, wear protective clothing (long pants, socks, sleeves) and use a tick repellent as directed.

In its early stages, Lyme disease may cause flulike symptoms and a reddish circular (bull's-eye) rash. If you have these symptoms or suspect you have been bitten by a tick, consult your prenatal caregiver without delay.

MARIJUANA

Most of the reasons not to smoke cigarettes during pregnancy (see "Smoking," page 108) also apply to smoking marijuana. Smokers have a greater risk of miscarriage, premature delivery, or stillbirth. In mothers who use marijuana, the placenta tends to be smaller and less efficient and their babies may be smaller and less well developed at birth than they would have been if the mother had not used the drug. There appears to be a strong link between marijuana use and behavioral abnormalities such as hyperactivity and irritability of the newborn. Although these problems may not persist beyond infancy, marijuana-induced behavioral abnormalities can make the first year difficult for both mother and baby.

MEDICATIONS (FOR LABOR AND DELIVERY) _____

Well before the day arrives, you should discuss with your prenatal care provider the issue of medication during labor and delivery. If you are attending childbirth preparation classes and intend to have an unmedicated labor and delivery, it's important that you and your caregiver communicate clearly about your expectations for this experience.

Ask your caregiver what would be available if you should require medication during labor or delivery. Analgesics relieve pain. Anesthetics temporarily deaden sensation, including pain. You should feel free to ask about the effects of any of these medications on your birthing experience and on your baby. It's best to talk about this before you go into labor so that there are no misunderstandings.

Special circumstances during your labor may, of course, present medical reasons for a change in plans. No matter how well informed or prepared you are, you and your birth attendants still may have to deal with the unexpected when the time comes. (See "Caesarean Delivery," pages 84–5, and "Epidural Anesthesia," page 91.)

MISCARRIAGE _____

Most early (first trimester) miscarriages are nature's way of dealing with a pregnancy resulting from a flawed ovum or sperm, or a pregnancy in which these cells joined incorrectly and could not develop normally. Factors that raise the chances of an early miscarriage include poor nutrition, environmental pollution or exposure to toxic substances, smoking, pelvic inflammatory disease, and infections such as chlamydia. A miscarriage later in pregnancy may be caused by a structural problem in the womb or cervix.

Difficult as it may seem, a woman who miscarries at home should try to save whatever tissue she can. Analysis of the tissue might shed light on what went wrong. If a miscarriage does not completely empty the womb, a brief hospitalization for a D and C (dilation and curettage) might be required.

More than half of the women who threaten to miscarry—that is, show one or more symptoms of a miscarriage—do not lose the pregnancy. For those who do lose the pregnancy in the first trimester, however, there is usually nothing that could have been done to change that outcome.

In some cases where a woman has had two or more unexplained miscarriages, current research suggests that it may be possible to find and treat the cause. Hormonal abnormalities, for example, may be a problem in up to 10 percent of recurrent miscarriages. If diagnosed, such problems can sometimes be treated successfully. A woman with the condition known as incompetent cervix, which typically causes a second trimester miscarriage, can have a successful pregnancy outcome if the condition is diagnosed early enough and the cervix stitched closed until shortly before term.

Immunological problems—situations in which the mother's immune system attacks the embryo, fetus, or placenta—are now thought to be responsible for many instances of multiple miscarriage. In some such cases, the mother's immune system malfunctions in a way that causes rejection of the embryo and fetus as foreign tissue. In other cases, the mother's body produces antibodies that cause clotting of placental blood, a condition that deprives the fetus of nutrients and oxygen. Recently developed treatments may enable many of these women to carry pregnancy to term and have a healthy baby.

Environmental hazards at home or in the workplace also have been associated with miscarriage (see "Household Hazards," pages 95–6; "Smoking," page 108; "Toxic Substances," pages 109–10; and "Workplace Hazards," pages 115–16).

Miscarriage can be a very difficult emotional experience for both parents. Grieving is appropriate and necessary as well as understandable. (See "Pregnancy Loss," page 102.) If a couple has experienced recurring miscarriages, genetic counseling and/or additional expert medical assistance should be sought to see if the problem is one for which help is available.

NONSTRESS TEST

The nonstress test, which measures fetal heart rate in relation to fetal movements, is used to provide information about the baby's well-being. In a nonstress test, a fetal heart monitor is used to measure the baby's heart rate over a period of time, perhaps thirty minutes or more. During this time, you will be asked to indicate each time you feel the baby move, or an attendant will note and keep track of fetal movements. Variability in fetal heart rate is looked for as the baby moves. Typically, heart rate will increase at such times.

Occasionally, a fetus will not move during the time of the nonstress test. While this may suggest a problem, it's also possible that the baby is simply taking a nap. If you have a nonstress test and your baby seems to be sleeping through it, your caregiver may use a buzzer as an alarm clock. Sometimes having the mother eat or drink something will rouse the fetus.

If the results of a nonstress test indicate the possibility of a problem, the test probably will be repeated and other diagnostic tools may be used (see "Biophysical Profile," page 82). In certain high risk cases, the results of a nonstress test may indicate a need to induce labor.

OVER-THE-COUNTER MEDICATIONS

Many medications, even the most ordinary everyday ones you can buy over the counter, go through the placenta to your baby and may cause harm. For example, aspirin—hardly a dangerous drug under normal circumstances—can be a hazard during pregnancy. Many cough and cold remedies contain ingredients, such as alcohol, that should be avoided during pregnancy. Diet pills, which should never be taken during pregnancy, may contain a stimulant known to be associated with birth defects.

During pregnancy, it's best not to take the potential safety of any drug or medication for granted, even if you have routinely purchased and used it in the past. Many suggestions for safely dealing with normal and typical problems of the pregnant condition can be found in section two, "Coping with Bodily Changes" (pages 21–36). For any discomfort you might have, there may be a number of suggested alternatives that can help you. If you feel the need for additional measures, homeopathic remedies (available in health food stores and from mail-order sources) may help enhance your body's own coping and healing abilities. Homeopathic remedies are nontoxic and safe for both mother and baby. For further information about homeopathic remedies, you can contact Homeopathic Educational Services, 2124 Kittredge Street, Berkeley, Calif. 94704. Telephone (510) 649-0294.

Before taking any over-the-counter preparation during pregnancy, you should be sure it's both safe and necessary to do so. Read labels and package inserts carefully. Ask your prenatal care provider for advice. During pregnancy, it's best to avoid any over-the-counter drug or medication unless your prenatal care provider suggests a particular product for a particular circumstance. Pregnancy is not the time to self-medicate.

PREECLAMPSIA (TOXEMIA) _____

Preeclampsia, also known as toxemia of pregnancy, is a disease that can be very dangerous for a pregnant woman and her baby. Symptoms of the disease include swelling of body tissues with rapid weight gain, high blood pressure, and protein (albumin) in the urine. Any two of these symptoms in combination indicate that a serious problem may be developing. In severe cases, there may be a marked drop in the amount of urine produced, abdominal pain, or blurred vision.

Despite considerable research on the subject, experts do not agree on the exact cause of toxemia of pregnancy. They do agree, however, that the best cure is prevention. Each time you visit your prenatal care provider, your blood pressure, urine, and weight will be checked and compared to what was recorded at your previous appointment. A physical exam will detect inappropriate fluid retention or swelling. In its mild or early stages, preeclampsia can be controlled. In cases where treatment is lacking or unsuccessful, the symptoms get more severe as time goes on.

Regular, sensible exercise (such as a brisk daily walk throughout pregnancy) may help prevent preeclampsia by promoting good circulation and reducing fluid retention. If symptoms of preeclampsia appear to be developing, bed rest may be prescribed to keep them under control. Don't lie on your back. Lying on the left side will best aid blood flow to your kidneys so they can do their job. You might also try resting with your feet elevated. A pillow or two under the mattress at the foot of your bed can elevate your feet while you sleep. This may help. Note that the suggestions to take a regular brisk walk and to rest on your left side or with your feet up are not in conflict. The rest is essential, and the walking will help to promote better circulation. Your caregiver will discuss with you what would be the right combination of rest and activity for your situation.

Although the exact cause of preeclampsia is not fully understood, the problem does in some cases seem to be related to poor nutrition. Be sure that your diet includes the nutrients you need, especially enough protein and B vitamins. Drink plenty of water throughout the day. Although at one time it was thought that salt restrictions would help prevent toxemia, it is now known that this is not so. You may salt to taste in moderation (see pages 55 and 63).

One of the problems in controlling preeclampsia is that the mother feels little or no discomfort during the early stages of the disease. She may not take her caregiver's warning seriously until it's too late. Preeclampsia decreases blood flow through the placenta, and this causes the baby to suffer. Babies of toxemic mothers tend to be small in relation to the length of time they are carried. They have a greater chance of being stillborn. A severely toxemic woman is in danger of having convulsions (eclampsia), which could be fatal to her or her baby.

If your prenatal care provider tells you that you are developing symptoms of pre-eclampsia, it's important to pay attention even if you think you feel fine. If it appears that the problems of preeclampsia are getting out of hand, hospitalization may be ordered.

PREGNANCY LOSS

While the majority of pregnancies end successfully for both mother and baby, some do not. You need not (and should not) dwell on the thought that something might go wrong. Your energies are better spent taking the best possible care of yourself and thinking positive thoughts. Nevertheless, it's not inappropriate for expectant parents to give some thought to how they might cope if they do suffer a miscarriage, stillbirth, or neonatal death. Chances are you won't need the information that follows this paragraph, but we've included it for those who do.

In times past, pregnancy loss was virtually an unmentionable subject, and the baby's remains were disposed of speedily because it was thought that this would be easiest for the parents. We now know, however, that such an approach is unwise. Today, parents who lose a child through miscarriage or stillbirth are encouraged to face and acknowl-edge the loss directly, to talk about it, and to grieve as they would in the death of any other close family member. It is suggested that parents name their baby and participate in a religious or memorial service if they wish to do so. If the baby is fully formed, the parents should see and hold the child. Many of those who do not see and hold their baby express regrets later. If a woman must remain in the hospital after losing a child, she should, if at all possible, be treated somewhere other than the maternity-nursery area where she would have to watch happy families with their babies.

Those who suffer a pregnancy loss may find comfort and support from others who themselves have experienced the death of an unborn or very young baby. Your prenatal caregiver may be able to direct you to a support group in your area. If not, you might contact SHARE, a clearinghouse for support groups for those who have experienced miscarriage or stillbirth. Approximately 240 groups across the country have registered with SHARE, and there may be one near you. Additional information can be obtained by writing to National SHARE Office, St. Joseph's Health Center, 300 First Capitol Drive, St. Charles, Mo. 63301, or calling (314) 947-6164.

PREP

A prep is the shaving of the pubic and perineal area or just the perineum (miniprep). For decades, prepping a laboring woman prior to delivery was a widely practiced hospital routine. It was believed that this procedure would reduce the risk of infection. Research has shown, however, that the rate of infection is lower among those women who have *not* been shaved. This is probably because the shaving can nick and abrade the skin, thereby leaving openings for bacteria. For a woman with very long hair on the perineum, a scissor clip might be recommended as an alternative.

A few caregivers may still order preps, but most no longer do so. Prepping is a procedure many women now choose to refuse. Discuss your wishes with your caregiver in advance.

PREPARED CHILDBIRTH

If at all possible, you and your partner should plan to attend a series of childbirth preparation classes. Most expectant parents begin classes in the seventh month (start of the third trimester), but it's a good idea to select a program and sign up earlier. Your prenatal care provider can direct you to classes available in your area.

The major childbirth preparation approaches from which to choose include the Dick-Read natural childbirth method, Bradley's "husband-coached childbirth," the Lamaze method, and Kitzinger's "touch relaxation" techniques. Many childbirth educators offer an eclectic approach that combines aspects of more than one method.

The Dick-Read ("childbirth without fear") method was the pioneering approach to natural childbirth in the United States. Introduced at a time when fully medicated labors were the norm and fathers were not permitted in the delivery room, the Dick-Read method originally relied on the medical staff (doctor/midwife/nurse) to provide emotional support for a woman in labor. Now, however, in keeping with current trends, the father is seen as an important member of the team throughout pregnancy and the birthing process.

The Lamaze method, based on Pavlov's theory of conditioned reflex, trains a woman to respond to the stimulus of a contraction with the conditioned reflex of relaxation

PREPARED CHILDBIRTH CLASSES	
DATE	TEACHER — TOPIC

rather than the instinctive response of tension, fear, and pain. A partner—either the child's father or some other person with whom the mother feels comfortable—acts as labor coach.

Bradley's method stresses a completely "natural" and unmedicated delivery. The child's father plays an important role during the pregnancy as well as the child's birth, and parents who choose the Bradley method of prepared childbirth may begin attending classes earlier than those who select another type of class. Some of the techniques used in Bradley's husband-coached childbirth were derived from observations of the instinctive behavior of animals during labor and delivery.

Kitzinger's method of childbirth preparation, which is very popular in England, places strong emphasis on the emotional and psychological aspects of childbearing as well as on body awareness and relaxation techniques.

The type of classes you attend will, of course, depend on what is convenient and available for you as well as which approach you favor. Even if you think your preference is for an unprepared, medicated labor and delivery, classes are recommended. The information gained will help you and your partner participate in your baby's birth in the way that is best for all of you.

In childbirth preparation classes, you will learn facts about labor and delivery that will help you to deal with it. You will learn to work with your body using special relaxation, controlled-breathing, and pushing techniques. Your partner will learn how to assist you. If your partner cannot or will not attend classes, it's still a good idea for you to go. What you learn will help you to work with your birth attendants during your labor and delivery.

Do not avoid classes because you fear that you might fail. No amount of preparation can guarantee that your labor and delivery will go exactly as expected. Attending classes does not commit you to doing things in a particular way once the time comes. The goal of classes is meaningful participation as well as performance. What you learn will increase the choices available to you.

PRESCRIPTION DRUGS AND MEDICINES

The placenta does not act as a barrier between your baby and the drugs or medications you take. Because a physician previously prescribed something for you does not mean that it is safe to continue taking the substance during pregnancy, although it may be safe. It's important that your prenatal care provider know exactly what prescription medications you have taken in the recent past and which, if any, you might need to continue. If you have a medical condition that requires treatment or maintenance doses of a pharmaceutical drug, it's important that your prenatal care provider works with you and the prescribing physician to achieve the optimum balance between your medical needs and the safety of your unborn child.

A list of commonly used medications and their possible effects during pregnancy should be available from your prenatal caregiver. Don't be afraid to ask. Unless you are sure that your prenatal care provider recommends a particular medication for you at this time, you should take nothing.

Rh-NEGATIVE MOTHERS _____

The blood test done early in pregnancy will indicate whether or not a mother's blood contains the Rh factor. If it does, the blood is described as Rh positive (Rh +). If not, it is called Rh negative (Rh −).

If your blood is Rh − and the baby's father has Rh + blood, the child may inherit the Rh factor from him and be Rh +, too. This would make your blood incompatible with that of your baby. As a result, your body may produce antibodies to protect itself from this "foreign" substance. The antibodies may be strong enough to attack the Rh + blood of a child in a future pregnancy.

Fortunately, there is a solution to the problem of an Rh − mother and an Rh + baby. Within seventy-two hours of delivery of an Rh + child, the mother must receive an injection of Rh immune globulin (called RhoGAM). An Rh − woman who has an abortion or miscarriage of an Rh + child would also need the injection. Use of RhoGAM in this way protects future unborn children by preventing antibodies from forming in the mother's blood.

In a small number of Rh − women, antibodies may be produced during pregnancy as well as after delivery. An injection of RhoGAM during week twenty-eight of the pregnancy can prevent this problem. Because there is no way to predict in advance which cases will need such treatment, many prenatal care providers recommend that *all* Rh- women receive RhoGAM during pregnancy as a precaution. This procedure is safe for both mother and fetus. Another dose of RhoGAM after delivery would be needed if the baby has Rh + blood.

If you are Rh +, there is no need for you to worry about any of this. If you and the baby's father are both Rh −, again there is no need for concern. The problem arises only with an Rh − mother and an Rh + baby.

RUBELLA _____

A woman who develops rubella (German measles) during the first three months of pregnancy has as great as a fifty-fifty chance of having a baby with severe problems such as brain damage, blindness, deafness, or heart and circulatory system defects. Prenatal rubella infection also can result in a child with delayed language or motor development and learning disabilities. The earlier in pregnancy the fetus is infected with rubella, the greater the risk of severe and multiple defects.

At your first prenatal visit, your blood probably was tested to find your level of immunity to rubella. If you have never had rubella and you are not immune, be extra careful not to be near anyone with an active case of the disease. Fortunately, as more and more preschool children are routinely immunized, the occurrence of rubella is becoming increasingly rare. Nevertheless, caution is in order. If you think you may have been exposed to rubella (or any other contagious disease), consult your prenatal caregiver without delay.

SAUNAS AND HOT TUBS _____

Exposure to extreme heat during early pregnancy may increase the risk of bearing a child with a neural tube defect. For this reason, pregnant women should not use saunas, hot tubs, steam rooms, or tanning salons. Even when taking a regular tub bath, you should be careful that the temperature of the water is not higher than 100°F. Especially during the first three months, soaking in very hot water or exposure to a strong dry heat source (such as a sauna or a tanning salon) can result in fetal damage.

Don't panic or feel guilty if you used a sauna or hot tub before you knew you were pregnant or before you found out that it might cause harm. Although the risk of fetal damage may have increased, it is still small. And now that you know, you can avoid the hot soaks and saunas for the rest of your pregnancy. An alpha fetoprotein test (see page 79) may be suggested. Chances are, the results will be reassuring.

SEXUALLY TRANSMITTED DISEASES _____

Sexually transmitted (venereal) diseases are a serious health problem in today's world. Certain of these diseases can cause harm or even death to a developing fetus. It's important for a pregnant woman who suspects she might have been infected to tell her prenatal care provider immediately so that the disease can be identified and treatment started.

During an early prenatal visit, a routine blood test will be used to check for syphilis, a disease that can cause a variety of defects as well as death of an unborn child. Some syphilis-related disorders may not appear until many years later. If the routine blood test is positive, further testing will be done to see what treatment is required. If identified promptly, syphilis usually can be cured completely.

Most prenatal care providers now test routinely for chlamydia, which has become the most common sexually transmitted disease. Although up to 80 percent of the women infected with chlamydia may show no symptoms, an infant who becomes infected with chlamydia in the birth canal may develop pneumonia or infections of the eyes, ears, stomach, or intestines. (See "Chlamydia," page 85.)

Many women with chlamydia also have gonorrhea. As with chlamydia, a woman may notice no symptoms of gonorrhea, although her baby can be infected in the birth canal. If a woman has gonorrhea at the time of labor and delivery and her baby is infected during passage through the birth canal, the baby may become blind. For this reason, most states require that medication (antibiotic ointment or silver nitrate drops) be routinely applied to babies' eyes soon after birth to prevent infection. Gonorrhea is curable and can be treated with antibiotics.

Herpes virus (type 2) is becoming increasingly common. During its active stage, this virus causes painful sores on the genitals. There is no known cure for genital herpes at this time, although the symptoms can be controlled and some relief provided. Because a newborn who contracts herpes in the birth canal is at considerable risk of death or serious defect, delivery by Caesarean section is indicated for a woman with an active case of genital herpes. (See page 94 for additional suggestions on dealing with the herpes virus.)

Acquired immune deficiency syndrome (AIDS) is showing a marked increase among women of childbearing age, especially those who have used intravenous drugs or who have had multiple partners. A woman who is carrying the AIDS virus (that is, one who tests HIV-positive) or who has been diagnosed as having AIDS is at high risk during pregnancy and at any other time. She and her baby require special monitoring and care. (See "AIDS," page 78.)

If you suspect that you might have a sexually transmitted disease, be sure to tell your prenatal caregiver without delay. Don't let embarrassment keep you from getting help when you need it. Your health and your baby's life may depend on it. To prevent infection or reinfection during pregnancy, some care providers suggest use of a condom during sexual activity. If you have a sexually transmitted disease and undergo treatment, in order to solve the problem it may be necessary to treat your partner as well.

SIBLING PARTICIPATION

Some families wish their children to be present at the birth of a new family member. Many alternative birth centers and some hospitals do permit siblings to be present at delivery. This practice, however, may not be appropriate or comfortable for many families, and you needn't feel that you are depriving your older children of an essential experience if you decide to leave them home. Here are some points to keep in mind if you do plan to have your other children with you during labor and delivery.

- Make sure the children are prepared for the experience and really want to be there. Your decision to have them present should meet their needs as well as your own.
- A responsible adult who is not your labor coach/companion should accompany each child and be prepared to leave the scene with him or her if necessary.
- Make arrangements with your birth attendants in advance for sibling participation. Don't show up in labor with an unannounced family entourage and expect everything to go according to your wishes. If the presence of your other children at delivery is very important to you, this may influence your choice of birth setting.

Most hospitals will make some provision for your children to visit their mother and new sister or brother after the baby is born. Find out ahead of time what procedures are followed in the place where you plan to give birth. Most families find that a sibling visit to the nursery and a chance for children to see their mother are worth the effort.

SMOKING

Smoking during pregnancy can be very harmful to your unborn child as well as to yourself and those around you. Recent studies indicate that the dangers of smoking are not limited to smokers. Passive smoking—breathing the air containing other people's smoke—can harm you and your baby in much the same manner as would your own smoking.

> **Warning: The Surgeon General Has Determined**
> **That Cigarette Smoking Is Dangerous to Your Health.**
> **Smoking During Pregnancy Can Cause Fetal Damage.**

Cigarette smoke introduces carbon monoxide, nicotine, and tar to your bloodstream. This cuts down on available oxygen for your baby and reduces the ability of the placenta to pass on nutrients and to get rid of wastes. The body of someone who smokes is less able to use nutrients such as folic acid, vitamins B_1, B_6, B_{12}, and C, and calcium, and so the baby is shortchanged in this way as well.

A pregnant woman who smokes increases her risk of placenta previa (abnormal placement of the placenta in the uterus) and other placental abnormalities. The baby of a mother who smokes is likely to be smaller and less well developed at birth than the baby of a mother who does not smoke. Smoking mothers tend to have more frequent miscarriages, premature deliveries, and stillbirths than women who do not smoke. Pregnant smokers may be at greater risk for complications during delivery, including those leading to the need for a Caesarean section.

Babies of smokers are more vulnerable to respiratory problems and diseases of early infancy and are more likely to die in infancy. If one or both of the parents smoke, the risk of crib death, or sudden infant death syndrome (SIDS), is greater than it would be in a nonsmoking household.

Smoking—whether you do it or those around you do it—is not good for you or your baby. If you or your baby's father have been unable to stop smoking for your own sake, perhaps the welfare of your unborn child will be the extra incentive you need to do it now.

SPORTS

Unless you're a surfer, diver, water skier, or football player, you may continue all of your customary athletic activities during pregnancy. It's best to stay away from team contact sports and potentially violent water sports in which a fall or pounding surf could force water up your vagina, but most other sports are fine. You need limit yourself only when *you* notice discomfort beyond what is normal for you.

To avoid the further straining of joints already strained by your pregnancy, warm up slowly and thoroughly before engaging in strenuous activity. As your pregnancy progresses, you'll have to make adjustments to accommodate your changing center of balance and new size and shape.

Stay with those physical activities to which your body was accustomed prior to your pregnancy. This is not the time to take up a new sport, especially one in which your lack of skill could add to the risk. For example, horseback riding or skiing might be fine if that has been a part of your regular routine up to now, but don't get on a horse or skis if you've never done it before. And even if you're an experienced and competent rider, skier, or whatever, you should take sensible precautions. No matter how good a rider you might be, for example, pregnancy is probably not a good time to school a young horse or jump big fences. And even an advanced skier might do better to limit herself to the easy slopes once her altered center of gravity has increased the likelihood of a fall.

Most people are able to do whatever they have been used to doing—jogging, biking, hiking, tennis, swimming, riding, or whatever—as long as they feel up to it and it makes sense to them. Unless there is some special problem with your pregnancy, you can continue most sports as long as you wish. If you would like specific guidance about appropriate activities for you, feel free to consult your prenatal care provider. What is comfortable for one person may be quite unsuitable for another. So, within reason, you're probably the best judge of what's right for you.

TAMPONS

Most people find that a minipad provides enough protection from the common vaginal discharge experienced during pregnancy. If you do not find a pad comfortable and feel that you must use a tampon, check with your prenatal care provider. For any tampon user, pregnant or not, we suggest the following guidelines:

- Do not use tampons containing perfume or deodorant.
- Do not use any tampon that has been chemically treated to increase absorbency.
- Be careful not to nick or cut yourself with the tampon's applicator, because this could leave openings for bacteria.
- Change the tampon frequently, and be sure your hands are clean before you do so. It's best not to leave a tampon in longer than four hours.

TOXIC SUBSTANCES

Although you should at all times try to avoid unnecessary contact with toxic substances in your environment, such care is especially important during pregnancy. It may surprise you to learn that some of the products you use routinely are potentially hazardous. Read labels carefully. If the label contains a warning about avoiding eye or skin contact, use the product with great care, if at all. If the label indicates that you should use the product only in a well-ventilated area, it probably would be better still if you didn't use it.

- Use household cleaners (especially those that produce fumes) only in well-ventilated areas. Don't inhale them. Avoid unnecessary exposure to cleaning chemicals such as dusting sprays and bathroom tile cleaners. Try nontoxic cleaning alternatives such as white vinegar, baking soda, lemon juice, salt, borax, or club soda.
- Avoid the use of aerosol containers whenever possible, and never use an aerosol can in a poorly ventilated place. If you shop carefully, you'll probably find that most of the products you would buy in a spray can have a non-aerosol alternative.
- Minimize any contact with insecticides, pesticides, weed killers, and similar substances in your home or garden. If you feel you must kill or control with chemicals, it's best to have someone else do the work for you.
- No matter how eager you might be to refinish baby furniture or paint the nursery, don't use paint removers or solvents while you are pregnant. If you insist on using such substances despite the risks, choose the least volatile you can find and be sure to work in a well-ventilated place. Latex-base paints are safer than oil-base paints. Letting another person do the painting while you're somewhere else is safest of all.
- Be cautious about personal items such as cosmetics, permanent-wave solutions, and hair dyes. Read the list of ingredients carefully. Stay away from products containing lead, mercury, or arsenic.

(See also "Household Hazards," pages 95–6, and "Workplace Hazards," pages 115–16.)

TOXEMIA OF PREGNANCY (SEE "PREECLAMPSIA")

TOXOPLASMOSIS

Toxoplasmosis is a flulike illness caused by protozoa. The disease in an adult is often so mild that it passes virtually unnoticed, but it can be extremely harmful—even fatal—for a fetus. When contracted by a pregnant woman, toxoplasmosis can result in severe brain or liver damage for her unborn child. Another effect toxoplasmosis may have on a fetus is damage to the retina of the eye, resulting in severe visual impairment or blindness. Any child who contracts toxoplasmosis in the womb is at risk for visual problems. These visual handicaps may show up immediately in an affected infant or they may not develop until years later.

Cats and raw meat are the two common sources of *toxoplasma gondii*, the tiny parasites that cause the disease. Fortunately, it's easy to minimize your chances of exposure.

- If you have a cat, get someone else to clean the litter box. If you have an outdoor cat, wear gloves when you garden or do yard work. Avoid any contact whatsoever with cat feces.
- While you are pregnant, the meat you eat should be thoroughly cooked. Omit steak tartare and very rare hamburgers from your menu until after your baby is born.

TRAVEL

Travel during pregnancy is fine. Being pregnant is not a reason to keep you home if there's somewhere you want or need to go.

Sitting still for long periods in a car, bus, plane, or train can slow down your circulation, so it's important to move around whenever you can. Stretch your arms, legs, and body from time to time. Get up and walk around for a few minutes each hour or two. If you are driving, pull over and get a bit of exercise before hitting the road again (see "Automobile Safety," pages 81–2).

Here are some things to keep in mind if you plan to travel by air while you are pregnant:

- Some airport security personnel permit a pregnant passenger to skip the electronic security check and be screened by a person instead. Ask.
- Fasten the seat belt loosely—across your lap and under your protruding abdomen.
- An aisle seat will be more convenient, because you'll be getting up often to move around and to use the lavatory.
- Eat and drink sensibly en route. You don't have to consume something just because a flight attendant puts it in front of you. Some airlines permit you to order special meals (for example, vegetarian or low-salt meals, or a sandwich) when you make the reservation.
- Avoid dehydration by drinking plenty of water.
- While seated, try to elevate your feet if possible. Pillows placed at the small of your back may make you more comfortable.
- Wear comfortable, nonbinding clothing. Your feet and legs may swell more than usual during a long flight. If you take off your shoes, you may have trouble putting them back on when you land.
- In the unlikely event of a rapid change in cabin pressure at high altitude, immediate use of supplemental oxygen would be essential for a pregnant woman.

If you travel by air when you are visibly pregnant, check in advance with the airline to find out if there are any special regulations. The rules vary greatly from one airline to another. Some airlines restrict travel during the week before the due date. Others ban it for the last month or more. Some may require a doctor's certificate. Others will take your word for it. An overzealous airline employee may not let you board if you appear to be close to delivery. This could happen even if your prenatal care provider thinks it's fine for you to travel. It's best to check on these details before you make final plans for a trip.

As your due date nears, unnecessary travel that involves great distances is not recommended, because labor may begin in an inconvenient place.

TWINS _____

Twins occur about once in ninety births. Identical twins are from a single fertilized ovum that splits completely very early in pregnancy and then develops into two babies. Fraternal twins develop from two different fertilized eggs. Because they have identical chromosome distribution, identical twins have the same sex, blood type, appearance, and other inherited characteristics. Fraternal twins, on the other hand, may be as alike or as different as any two children of the same parents.

If your prenatal caregiver finds that your uterus is increasing in size more rapidly than would be expected, a multiple pregnancy may be the reason. Locating two separate fetal heartbeats could confirm the diagnosis. An ultrasound examination (see page 112), which can provide definite information about the number of babies a woman is carrying, will probably be done as soon as possible.

If you are having more than one baby, you may notice some of the possible discomforts of pregnancy more strongly than someone who is carrying only one child. Paying close attention to the suggestions for coping with bodily changes, pages 21–36, may be helpful. Ask your prenatal caregiver if there are any modifications to these suggestions required for your particular situation.

Premature delivery is a frequent complication associated with multiple births. Because of this, a woman known to be carrying twins or more might need extra rest or special precautions during the last three months or so of pregnancy. If this is necessary in your case, your caregiver will advise you. Be sure to communicate your concerns to him or her and ask any questions you might have.

ULTRASOUND _____

Ultrasound is a diagnostic tool that uses high-frequency sound waves to create pictures of the fetus. Ultrasound can provide pictures, called sonograms, that show soft tissue in considerable detail. Real-time is a continuous ultrasound that shows motion and can be seen on a TV monitor. It also can be recorded in still frames using a Polaroid camera.

An ultrasound exam, or sonogram, as it is commonly called, is a relatively simple procedure that typically takes only a few minutes. The examiner uses a small, hand-held device called a transducer, which is moved back and forth across the woman's abdomen. The transducer sends out sound waves that, as they bounce off the fetus, create an image on the monitor.

A recently developed type of ultrasound uses a transducer that is inserted in the woman's vagina rather than being moved externally across the abdomen. Transvaginal ultrasound provides pictures of very early fetal development that may not be obtainable using traditional ultrasound. It is especially useful, therefore, in early pregnancy.

There are a number of different purposes for which ultrasound is used. It can be used to determine the age and size of the fetus, and it may be ordered in midpregnancy if there is some question about the actual due date. A sonogram can show the location of the placenta, the presence of certain abnormalities, and multiple fetuses. In some instances, a sonogram may also indicate the sex of the fetus.

If you have amniocentesis, ultrasound will be used to locate the precise location of the fetus and the placenta, to enable the examiner to know exactly where to insert the needle to withdraw amniotic fluid.

Ultrasound is a useful diagnostic technique that should be employed when the information it can obtain is necessary or useful to provide for your well-being or that of your baby. There are no known harmful effects. The long-term effects of ultrasound, if any, have not been studied and are not known at this time. It may be wise, therefore, to avoid routine or unnecessary sonograms. If your prenatal care provider suggests a sonogram for you, feel free to ask any questions you might have about the indications for it or the interpretation of the results.

VAGINAL BIRTH AFTER CAESAREAN (VBAC) __

Until recently, any woman who had a baby by Caesarean section could count on having future children that way as well. Now the practice of routine repeat Caesareans is changing, as more and more women are demanding an opportunity to attempt VBAC (pronounced vee-back) and more and more care providers are willing to give them that chance.

If your previous Caesarean used a low horizontal uterine incision, a vaginal delivery may be as safe for your baby as a repeat Caesarean, and it may be even safer for you. Here are some suggestions to help you achieve a vaginal birth after Caesarean if at all possible for your particular circumstances.

- Find a supportive obstetrician who is willing to attempt VBAC and who is actively committed to helping you succeed.

- Be sure to attend childbirth preparation classes. Try to find an instructor who provides information and supportive instruction on VBAC. You may even be able to find a class especially geared toward preparation for VBAC.

- Consider hiring a nurse-midwife or monitrice to be with you during labor, especially if your obstetrician requires VBAC candidates to come to the hospital in early labor. The close personal support of a birth attendant who focuses on delivery as a normal process rather than a medical problem can help you get safely through a longer trial of labor than you might be able to manage on your own.

- For additional information, contact the International Cesarean Awareness Network, P.O. Box 152, University Station, Syracuse, N.Y. 13210. Telephone (315) 424-1942.

Even if you are well prepared and highly motivated and your birth attendants are supportive, it's possible that you'll require a repeat Caesarean anyway. There may be a new reason, unrelated to the earlier Caesarean, or a recurrence of the previous cause. If this should occur, remember that it doesn't mean you have failed. It simply means that a medical decision was made at the time of need rather than months earlier in anticipation of something that might never have happened.

WEIGHT

During pregnancy, a weight gain of twenty-four to thirty pounds is both normal and recommended. Unless your prenatal care provider specifically instructs you otherwise, this is what you should aim for. If you are eating nutritious food, your gain is not fat. Most of this weight can be lost within two to six weeks after you give birth.

For a typical mother who eats wisely during pregnancy, here's what the recommended twenty-four-pound gain might include:

Baby	7.5 pounds
Placenta	1.5 pounds
Amniotic fluid	2.0 pounds
Breast tissue	1.0 pounds
Uterus	2.5 pounds
Blood	3.5 pounds
Other fluid	2.75 pounds
Other	3.25 pounds

You will find guidelines for nutrition during pregnancy on pages 38–67. These pages describe the types of foods you should be eating and the reasons why. Do not diet to lose weight or even to maintain your previous weight level while you are pregnant. Your baby and your hardworking body need the recommended calories and nutrients. The recommended weight gain is essential to your baby's health.

How much you gain is important, but so is the rate at which you gain. A slow, steady increase during the second and third trimesters—about a pound every eight to ten days—is preferable to erratic weight changes. A typical weight gain of twenty-four to thirty pounds would be distributed as follows: three to four pounds during the first three months, ten to twelve pounds during the second three months, and eleven to fourteen pounds during the last three months.

WORKPLACE HAZARDS

Although a woman has a right to continue working throughout pregnancy if she is able to do so, there are hazards in some workplace environments that might make a decision to do so unwise. You should find out if the type of work you do may pose unusual risks for a fetus. If so, you should find out as much information as you can and discuss the matter with your prenatal care provider. Whatever decision you make should be an informed one.

Some workplace substances are definitely known to be teratogenic (that is, harmful to a fetus if the mother is exposed during pregnancy). Many other substances are of questionable safety, although research may be conflicting or inconclusive. The potential effect of a teratogen on a pregnancy depends on what the substance is, the duration and intensity of the exposure, and the point in a woman's pregnancy at which she encounters the substance.

Lead is a known teratogen. Workers exposed to lead or lead dust are at risk. Such workers may include those involved in paint manufacturing or painting; artists; printers;

those involved in glass blowing, ceramics, or pottery glazing; battery manufacturers; electronics workers; and anyone who works with solder or lead pipes. Although the use of unleaded gasoline has decreased the amount of airborne lead resulting from motor vehicles, laborers on heavily traveled roads and near service stations and toll booths may still encounter unacceptable amounts of lead as well as carbon monoxide from automobile emissions.

Health-care workers face various types of risks. Ionizing radiation (X rays) is hazardous. Radiologists and X-ray technicians should limit exposure. Health-care workers (nurses, doctors, pharmacists, physician's assistants) exposed to chemotherapy may face an increased risk of miscarriage and birth defects. Some health-care workers may face a variety of contagious or infectious diseases, some of which could cause harm to the fetus.

Teachers, day-care providers, and others whose work brings them in close contact with children must, like health care workers, be alert to the potential for exposure to contagious and infectious diseases. Although routine immunization protects today's children from many childhood diseases, there are still some ailments such as chicken pox or fifth disease that may be encountered in a school or daycare setting.

The unborn child of a pregnant woman who contracts chicken pox may actually develop pockmarks. If the disease has time to run its course before delivery, chances are the skin blemishes will have healed. A baby who contracts the infection just prior to or during delivery, before receiving maternal antibodies against the virus, however, is at high risk. Immediate medical intervention would be required to prevent serious complications. Any woman who did not have chicken pox as a child should try to avoid exposure to the disease during pregnancy. Fifth disease, a virus that causes fever, rash, and a flushed appearance, is a typically mild childhood disease that can, in rare instances, cause a problem to a fetus, especially during the first trimester. A pregnant woman who works with children should be alert to the possibility of an outbreak of fifth disease in those with whom she works. Avoidance of exposure, if at all possible, is prudent.

Women exposed to certain chemicals involved in microchip production have been found to be at significantly higher risk for miscarriage than are their colleagues elsewhere in the industry. These chemicals, glycol ethers, are also used in other industries, such as aerospace and printing. If you work in the semiconductor industry or any other in which hazardous chemicals are used, consult your caregiver to obtain the latest research information and specific counsel for your circumstances.

There is considerable controversy concerning the issue of nonionizing radiation—that is, radiation from such items as electric transmission lines, video display terminals, color television sets, and microwave ovens. Although there is a growing body of data suggesting a link between electromagnetic fields and childhood leukemia, proximity of your home or job to high-power transmission lines may not be something you can readily change. You should, however, be informed. Don't be afraid to ask your local utility for the latest research.

Studies on the potential hazards of video display terminals are confusing and conflicting. Some research indicates use of VDTs during pregnancy has no effect on the risk of miscarriage or birth defects. Others do find a link. Many prenatal guidebooks and pamphlets ignore the issue or simply say VDTs are safe. Unfortunately, the simple answers may not be the best. Although there is much data to suggest that VDT use during pregnancy does not cause miscarriage or other problems, some contrary claims seem quite compelling. One recent study reported triple the risk of miscarriage among women who used VDT models that emitted high levels of extremely low frequency electromagnetic field, although VDT use in general did not increase the miscarriage rate. In other words, the problem was caused by certain VDTs, not all of them.

Further research on the safety of VDTs is under way. If your job involves extensive exposure to a computer monitor, what does all this mean for you? Chances are, there won't be a problem. If you are concerned, however, you should feel free to ask questions about the type of VDT you are using and whether or not it has been linked to pregnancy risk. Shut off the monitor when it's not in use. Another problem of VDT use—one that has nothing to do with the electromagnetic field—involves sitting for long periods. Be sure to get up every hour or two and walk around to maintain good circulation. Try to sit in a way that does not strain your back and neck.

For additional information about VDT or other job-related hazards, you may call the 9 to 5 National Association of Working Women. Call the toll-free hotline at (800) 522-0925 or write to: 9 to 5, 614 Superior Avenue NW, Cleveland, Ohio 44113.

X RAYS

When you are pregnant, you should avoid X rays if at all possible. Postpone routine diagnostic X rays, such as those for nonessential dental work, until after your baby is born. If an emergency or a medical condition unrelated to your pregnancy should make it absolutely necessary for you to have an X ray, it's important that the prescribing physician and radiology staff know you are pregnant so that appropriate precautions can be taken in administering the procedure. Before allowing an X ray in circumstances other than a life-threatening emergency during your pregnancy, you may wish to obtain a second opinion.

BOOKS FOR YOUR INFORMATION _____

As you work with your prenatal care provider and prepared childbirth instructor throughout your pregnancy, you'll probably find that *While Waiting* contains the basic information you need on topics most important to your health and comfort. For further reading about pregnancy, childbirth, and newborn baby care, additional titles are suggested below.

Babysense: A Practical and Supportive Guide to Baby Care
Frances Wells Burck (New York: St. Martin's Press, 1991)

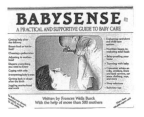

A reassuring guide for babycare during the first year, along with suggestions for a mother's postpartum recovery. More than five hundred parents contributed suggestions to this practical book, which has been completely revised and updated for the 1990s.

Beyond Jennifer and Jason: An Enlightened Guide to Naming Your Baby
Linda Rosenkrantz and Pamela Redmond Satran (New York: St. Martin's Press, 1990)

Categorizes names by style, image, sex, and tradition. Dubbed by the *Wall Street Journal* as "the arbiter of hip baby names." Interesting, although perhaps a bit trendy.

Birth Without Violence
Frederick Leboyer, M.D. (New York: Knopf, 1975; paperback, New York: Fawcett, 1990)

Beautifully written text and fine photographs focus on the baby's needs and feelings during the birth process. Leboyer makes a powerful case for a gentle birth that is worth reading even if you don't entirely agree with his ideas or methods.

Breastfeeding and the Working Mother
Diane Mason and Diane Ingersoll (New York: St. Martin's Press, 1986)

A complete handbook for mothers who want to breastfeed and continue working. Provides practical tips for mothers in every conceivable job situation—full time, part time, travel, meetings. The book also covers nursing dress, equipment, and legal rights. A useful guide whether or not you plan to work outside the home.

A Child Is Born
Lennart Nilsson (New York: Dell, 1990)

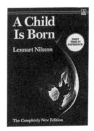

An unusual and worthwhile (although costly) addition to any home library. Fascinating color photographs of prenatal life provide information and help to communicate a sense of the mystery and beauty of a new life from the moment of conception. This completely new edition is now available in paperback.

Childbirth Without Fear: The Principles and Practices of Natural Childbirth
Grantly Dick-Read (5th ed., New York: Harper and Row, 1987)

The pioneer in introducing childbirth education and natural childbirth methods to the United States. The approach has evolved with changing trends and now actively involves the father as a major source of emotional support.

The Complete Book of Pregnancy and Childbirth
Sheila Kitzinger (rev. ed., New York: Knopf, 1987)

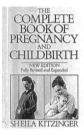

Comprehensive, beautifully written and illustrated. This revised and expanded edition of one of the best books we've seen can help you develop awareness and understanding of the childbearing process so you can fully and actively participate in the experience in the most joyful and satisfying way for yourself, your partner, and your baby.

Easing Labor Pain
Adrienne B. Lieberman (rev. ed., Boston: Harvard Common Press, 1992)

A handbook of strategies to deal with labor pain. This supportive book covers a wide range of possibilities—from acupuncture and biofeedback to Lamaze to medical intervention—and can help you choose the birthing plan that is best for you.

Essential Exercises for the Childbearing Year
Elizabeth Noble (Boston: Houghton Mifflin, 1988)

A comprehensive collection of exercises for fitness during pregnancy and for a rapid postpartum recovery. Drawings and diagrams illustrate the specific instructions.

The Experience of Childbirth
Sheila Kitzinger (New York: Penguin Books, 1990)

A guide to Kitzinger's touch-relaxation method of prepared childbirth. This book deals with the emotional as well as the physical aspect of childbearing.

A Good Birth, A Safe Birth
Diana Korte and Roberta Scaer (3d ed., Boston: Harvard Common Press, 1992)

Detailed information about today's trends in childbirth and the options available. This consumer-oriented volume can help you achieve the childbearing experience you wish in a hospital setting. Excellent bibliography and list of resources.

Having a Baby: A Complete Guide for the Mother-to-Be
Eric Trimmer, M.B., B.S., M.R.C.G.P. (New York: St. Martin's Press, 1981)

Contains a pregnant woman's nine-month diary illustrated with color photographs and a detailed presentation of information about pregnancy, delivery, and care of the newborn baby, along with suggestions for personal health care.

The Healthy Baby Book
Carolyn Reuben (New York: Jeremy P. Tarcher/Perigee Books, 1992)

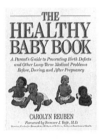

A parent's guide to preventing birth defects and other long-term medical problems before, during, and after pregnancy. This book is an excellent resource for coping with potential hazards of the modern world at home, in the workplace, in your diet and medical care, and in the general environment.

Homeopathy for Pregnancy, Birth, and Your Baby's First Year
Miranda Castro (New York: St. Martin's Press, 1993)

An interesting and reassuring volume that explains how to use homeopathic principles for your health and comfort during pregnancy and for caring for your newborn. This book is full of useful information and practical advice.

Husband-Coached Childbirth
Robert A. Bradley (3d ed., New York: Harper and Row, 1981)

Describes Bradley's method of prepared childbirth in which the father's participation throughout pregnancy and birth is stressed. Bradley's enthusiasm for this natural, nonmedicated, family-centered approach is evident in his writing.

Mientras Espera
George E. Verrilli, M.D., F.A.C.O.G., and Anne Marie Mueser, Ed.D. (New York: St. Martin's Press, 1988)

The complete, original edition of *While Waiting* for those who wish to use the Spanish language to obtain information they need about pregnancy-related topics.

The Nursing Mother's Companion
Kathleen Huggins, R.N., M.S. (rev. ed., Boston: Harvard Common Press, 1990)

A beautifully written and presented guide to every aspect of breastfeeding your baby. Supportive and sound information that will be reassuring as well as helpful.

Nurturing the Unborn Child
Thomas Verny, M.D., and Pamela Weintraub (New York: Dell, 1991)

A nine-month program for soothing, stimulating, and communicating with your baby. Based on current research in prenatal psychology, this fascinating book offers step-by-step suggestions for bonding with your unborn child.

The Parents' Guide to Raising Twins
Elizabeth Friedrich and Cherry Rowland (New York: St. Martin's Press, 1984; paperback, 1990)

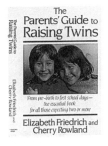

A useful book for those who suspect or know they are having more than one baby. The authors, both mothers of twins, write from personal experience as well as other research.

Pregnancy After 35
Carole Spearin McCauley (New York: Pocket Books, 1987)

A guide to prenatal care especially for women over the age of thirty-five but useful for others as well. The book contains sections on genetic counseling and on single parenting.

The Pregnancy Nutrition Counter
Annette B. Natow, Ph.D., R.D., and Jo-Ann Heslin, M.A., R.D. (New York: Pocket Books, 1992)

A useful book with more than 150 pages of charts to provide nutritional facts about virtually anything you might want to eat from A (abalone) to Z (zucchini).

The Premature Baby Book: A Parents' Guide to Coping and Caring in the First Years
Helen Harrison with Ann Kositsky, R.N. (New York: St. Martin's Press, 1983)

Contains a wealth of medical and practical information and support for parents of a premature baby. If your waiting ends significantly sooner than expected, this book is a must.

Preparation for Childbirth: A Lamaze Guide
Donna and Roger Ewy (New York: New American Library, 1982)

Presents detailed directions for breathing, relaxing, and conditioning exercises in preparation for childbirth. Includes clear instructions for the labor coach and mother.

Talk and Toddle: A Commonsense Guide for the First Three Years
Anne Marie Mueser, Ed.D., and Lynn M. Liptay, M.D. (New York: St. Martin's Press, 1983)

Before long, your newborn will be a mobile baby and then a toddler. This book is designed to help you cope with these demanding and exciting early years. Topics of concern to a toddler's parents are arranged alphabetically for easy reference.

Twins, Triplets and More
Elizabeth M. Bryan, M.D. (New York: St. Martin's Press, 1992)

A reassuring, common sense volume of supportive information about twins, triplets, and more from before birth through high school. This concise volume addresses the critical and unique concerns involved in multiple-birth parenting.

Welcome Baby: A Guide to the First Six Weeks
Anne Marie Mueser, Ed.D., and George E. Verrilli, M.D. (New York: St. Martin's Press, 1982)

Contains numerous helpful suggestions for the busy days and weeks after your new baby's arrival. This companion volume to *While Waiting* is presented in a similar easy-to-read format.

Yoga for Pregnancy: Safe and Gentle Stretches
Sandra Jordan (New York: St. Martin's Press, 1987; paperback, 1988)

Photographs and concise descriptions provide instruction for ninety-two safe and gentle stretches suitable for use by pregnant women and new mothers. This guide can help you achieve harmony of mind and body as you prepare for a relaxed labor and birth.

SECTION FIVE

LABOR AND DELIVERY

PRETERM LABOR

WHAT ARE THE WARNING SIGNALS FOR PRETERM LABOR?

For some women, backache and pelvic discomfort may be normal experiences of pregnancy. Persistent or rhythmic low back or pelvic pressure, however, especially if it feels different from what you've felt up to now, may be a warning signal. Cramps—either like those of a menstrual period or intestinal cramps with or without diarrhea—may signal a complication. An increase or change in vaginal discharge—especially if the discharge is clear and watery or tinged with blood—should be reported promptly to your caregiver.

WHAT IF LABOR STARTS TOO SOON?

Call your prenatal care provider immediately if you think you are experiencing any of the signs of labor sooner than you think you should. Be alert to the warning signals of pregnancy complications, and don't be afraid to call your prenatal care provider if you feel that something is not right. If you are truly in premature labor, it's important for you to receive medical attention without delay. If you are mistaken, your caution and concern will cause no harm.

Once preterm labor has begun, it may not be possible to stop the process. There are measures, however, including use of one or more labor-stopping drugs, that may be effective if employed soon enough. If preterm labor is effectively halted, bed rest and complete relaxation will be ordered to delay the recurrence of labor as long as possible. If labor can be delayed, a drug to hasten the baby's lung development may be administered.

If you experience premature labor, you may be directed to a nearby hospital with neonatal care facilities even if that's not the place you had planned to deliver. If your preterm labor can't be stopped, it's important that your premature infant be in a facility equipped to provide special care. Sometimes a high-risk infant is transferred by ambulance or helicopter to a special facility after delivery.

 IMPORTANT WARNING SIGNS

Any of the following may be warning signs that you are at risk for preterm labor and delivery. Call your prenatal care provider immediately and be prepared to go straight to the hospital if required.

- Persistent or rhythmic low back pain that feels different from what you are used to in this pregnancy
- Menstrual-like cramps
- Intestinal cramps with or without diarrhea
- Pelvic pressure or rhythmic tightening that feels different from what you are used to in this pregnancy
- Watery discharge or a gush of fluid from your vagina
- Vaginal bleeding.

YOUR BODY GETS READY

As your baby enters the birth canal, the mouth of your uterus (cervix) will thin out (efface) and open (dilate). This process of effacement and dilation may begin before you actually go into labor. At each of your prenatal care visits during the last month of pregnancy, you probably will be given an internal examination to check the effacement and dilation of your cervix and the descent (station) of your baby's presenting part.

The degree of effacement is reported in percents. For example, a cervix that has thinned out three-fourths of the way is said to be 75 percent effaced. Dilation is measured in centimeters or fingers. One finger equals approximately two centimeters.

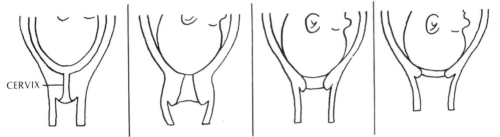

CERVIX

During the first stage of labor (see pages 128–32), the cervix effaces fully and dilates to about ten centimeters (five fingers) so the baby's head can get through. The first stage of labor ends when the cervix is fully effaced and dilated.

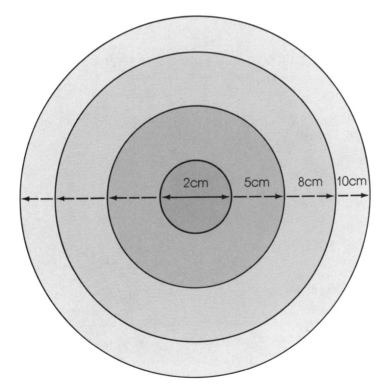

2cm   5cm   8cm   10cm

The progress of the baby's head as it descends through the pelvis during labor is reported in a number called a station. The station numbers range from -4 to $+4$. When the baby's head has not yet started its descent, the station is described as -4. When the baby's head is at zero station, it is at the midsection of the birth canal. When the descent of the head through the birth canal is completed, the station is identified as $+4$.

SIGNS OF LABOR

Any or all of these signs—contractions, rupture of membranes, bloody show—can signal the beginning of labor.

CONTRACTIONS

During the last weeks of pregnancy, you may from time to time feel contractions of your uterus. These contractions, called Braxton-Hicks contractions, prepare the muscles for labor but do not result in the baby's birth. They do not become stronger with time, and relaxation (try drinking a glass of warm milk) or a change in position usually relieves them.

The contractions of labor are different. When contractions come at regular intervals and increase in frequency, duration, and intensity as time progresses, you may be in labor. Lying down or relaxing will not stop or relieve the contractions of true labor. These contractions are characterized by a dull ache across the back that radiates around to the front. They may be accompanied by a sense of pressure in the pelvis.

CONTRACTIONS OF LABOR	BRAXTON-HICKS CONTRACTIONS
• occur at regular intervals	• are irregular and erratic
• increase in frequency as time passes (intervals between them shorten)	• occur at intervals that do not become shorter as time passes
• increase in duration as time passes	• do not increase in duration as time passes
• are not stopped by change in position or relaxation	• usually can be relieved by change in position or relaxation
• cause discomfort in back and lower abdomen with pelvic pressure	• cause discomfort mainly in lower abdomen, typically without pelvic pressure or backache
• become stronger and more intense as time passes	• do not cause the cervix to dilate

RUPTURE OF MEMBRANES

The rupture of membranes also is referred to as the breaking of the bag of waters. This is a sign that labor may be on the way. When the membranes rupture, fluid may escape in a sudden gush or trickle out in a slow leak. The fluid may be sticky and it is usually clear or slightly milky in appearance. It is essentially odorless and readily distinguishable from urine, although the woman whose bag of waters breaks may feel as if she has wet her pants. There is no pain when the membranes rupture, although some women say they sense a tiny "pop." The membranes do not always rupture early in labor, and it is possible for a baby to be born with the bag of waters still intact.

If your bag of waters breaks, you should notify your prenatal care provider. Although labor is likely to start soon (within the next few hours), it may not. Because there is increased danger of infection at this time, your caregiver may take the precaution of having you come to the hospital or birth center, where you can be watched and labor induced if necessary.

SHOW

The plug of mucus that closes off the entrance to the uterus during pregnancy may be expelled just prior to or during labor. This is a small mucous mass usually tinged with a little blood. It is often referred to as "show" or "bloody show." Although its appearance may suggest that labor is likely to begin soon, show is not a very reliable indicator.

WHEN THE BABY IS OVERDUE _____

HOW LONG IS TOO LONG?

If your expected due date has come and gone, you're likely to be somewhat anxious as well as certain you've been pregnant too long. When you feel as if the baby will never arrive, remember that the due date is only an estimate. Delivery two weeks earlier or later than the due date is considered on schedule. And there's always the possibility that an irregularity in your cycle might have caused a miscalculation. Chances are, you're not really overdue and your baby will arrive when he or she is ready. Nevertheless, a few women do not go into labor at term as they should. In such cases, intervention may be required to prevent the baby from being seriously postmature.

WHAT CAN BE DONE?

If you are more than two weeks past your expected due date and you show no signs of labor, there are steps your prenatal care provider might take to make sure avoidable problems are prevented. There are several tests that might be used to assess fetal well-being. Depending on the results of these tests, your caregiver might induce labor or deliver your baby by Caesarean section. Or you might be reassured that everything is in order and you should wait awhile longer. Feel free to ask questions and share your concerns with your care provider.

See "Amniocentesis," page 80; "Biophysical Profile," page 82; "Contraction Stress Test," page 86; "Induced Labor," page 97; "Nonstress Test," page 100; and "Ultrasound," page 112. You also might find this a good time to go back to page 3 and reread "When Is Your Baby Due?"

THE WAITING IS OVER _____

WHEN SHOULD YOU CALL YOUR CARE PROVIDER?

If you suspect that any of the signs of labor are happening and would like to discuss them with your prenatal care provider, feel free to call. If you are able, you should make the call yourself rather than having someone else make it for you. It's best for you to answer questions directly and explain exactly how you feel. A high-risk mother should notify her caregiver promptly when labor begins.

IMPORTANT PHONE NUMBERS
Caregiver: _____
Hospital/Birth Center: _____
Other: _____

When you call your care provider, he or she will discuss your condition with you on the phone and perhaps see you in the office for a labor check. The time you should leave for the hospital or birth center will depend on the particular circumstances of your case as well as on how you are feeling and how your labor is progressing.

Discuss with your care provider in advance what guidelines will be used for deciding when you should be admitted to the hospital or birth center. Be prepared to be flexible if unforeseen circumstances should result in a need to change your plans.

WHAT SHOULD YOU BRING?

Don't make elaborate preparations for your hospital or birth center stay. It's likely to be short. For labor and delivery, you'll probably wear a hospital gown. A pair of cotton socks might be helpful in case you get chilly feet during labor. In your prepared childbirth classes, you may have developed a list of items to pack. Bring whatever snacks and fluids you will need during labor as well as things for your partner to eat and drink. This is especially important if you'll be in labor at a time the cafeteria is closed. Leave expensive jewelry at home.

For your stay in maternity, you'll need clothing to keep you comfortable and covered as you wander between your room and the nursery or lounge. Bring something—slippers or moccasins—for your feet. If you're going to breastfeed, be sure whatever you wear opens easily in the front. A lightweight robe with a front zipper is very handy. Don't forget your nursing bras—at least two. Bring your toothbrush, comb, and whatever makeup you'll want to use. If you're reading a good book, bring that, too. Don't make a big deal out of packing. Someone can bring you the things you've forgotten.

Delivery won't restore you instantly to your prepregnancy size and shape, so pack a loose-fitting garment for your trip home.

HOW DO YOU SIGN IN?

If your prenatal care provider knows you are on the way, it's likely that the hospital or birth center will have been notified to expect you. You should find out ahead of time which entrance to use, what the admissions procedures are, and what financial arrangements are necessary. These are not matters you'll want to spend time figuring out when you are well along in labor, particularly if it's the middle of the night.

WHAT HAPPENS NEXT?

After being admitted to the hospital or birth center, you will go to the place where you are to spend your time in labor. In a hospital setting using traditional labor, delivery, and recovery rooms, you will be sent to the labor area. If you plan to labor and deliver in a private birthing room, you will go directly there.

Your labor nurse probably will give you a hospital gown to put on. She will ask you for a urine sample. If you have not had a recent bowel movement, an enema (see page 91) may be suggested. If a prep (see page 102) has been ordered and you agree, it would be done at that time. If you have any questions about the procedures, you should ask. If certain routine procedures are not a part of your personal plans or preference, it's best to discuss your wishes with your care provider before you enter the hospital in labor.

In many birth settings, it is possible for your partner to remain with you at all times, although staff in some hospitals prefer not to permit this. If you feel strongly about avoiding any separation from your partner, this is another point to discuss with your birth attendant before the time comes. If you and your partner must be separated for any reason, be sure he knows where he will be able to find you again.

The labor nurse will listen to your baby's heartbeat. Your temperature may be taken and your blood pressure will be checked. An internal examination probably will be done at that time to see how your labor is progressing.

If you and your care provider have agreed to continuous monitoring using an electronic fetal monitor, the monitoring device will be set up. If you are not going to be attached to an electronic fetal monitor, your baby's heartbeat will be checked frequently with a hand-held device. As your labor continues, you will be given an internal exam from time to time to check your progress.

If you are going to have your baby in the delivery room, you will be moved there a few minutes before the baby is to be born. If you are in a birthing room, you will stay right where you are. For a detailed description of the stages of labor, see pages 127–34.

GUIDELINES FOR LABOR AND DELIVERY _____

The following guidelines for labor and delivery are based on the reported experiences of many women. These descriptions will acquaint you with a typical labor and delivery and give you some idea of what might be in store. Do not, however, expect your labor to duplicate exactly what is described here. You may not experience all of the reactions listed and you may have some that are not mentioned.

The suggestions outlined here are very brief. They are not intended to replace classes for prepared childbirth or directions from your caregivers. Reading this material should not make you feel that you must diagnose your own progress or that you have in some way failed if your labor does not fit the norm. No matter how well prepared you and your partner may be, you would do well to seek the guidance of your birth attendants, who will help you meet the personal demands of your particular situation as it evolves.

FIRST STAGE OF LABOR: 0 TO 2–3 CM DILATION

WHAT'S HAPPENING

The contractions are rhythmic and get stronger as time progresses. Women have described these contractions in a number of different ways: pelvic pressure, backache, like menstrual cramps, gas, tightening in the area of the pubic bone. This stage of labor may be accompanied by bloody show and/or rupture of the membranes. Some women feel chilly or experience nausea at this time. For most women, this stage is the longest in comparison to the others. It may last several hours.

REACTIONS OF MOTHER

Most women feel excited and relieved that labor is at last under way, although these feelings are often accompanied by some measure of anxiety. Many women feel quite sociable at this stage and carry on conversation between contractions.

WHAT TO DO

- Indulge in activities to keep your mind off the contractions. Read, watch television, play a table game, do a crossword puzzle, or find something else to do around the house that will keep you busy as long as you feel able.
- If it's nighttime or if you're tired, it's fine to try to sleep. If you can't sleep, don't worry about it.
- This is not a good time for a multicourse meal, but if you're hungry, you may eat something. Labor is hard work, and you'll have to keep up your energy level.
- Prevent dehydration by keeping up your fluid intake. Nourishing fluids are useful, especially if you don't feel like eating solid food. Soups, juices, or milkshakes can help meet your need for fluids and give you energy.
- If you think the contractions are six to seven minutes apart or less, time them. Keep track of how often they occur and how long each one lasts.

HINTS FOR HELPING

- Encourage and share activities to keep her mind off the contractions.
- If she wants to rest, encourage her to do so.

- Take a walk with her.
- Encourage her to eat sensibly and lightly if she's hungry. Make sure she keeps up her fluid intake. Make tea or herb tea with honey (or sugar) if she doesn't feel like eating or having soup.
- Don't suggest timing the contractions until they are six to seven minutes apart or less. If they are farther apart than this, you shouldn't be in a hurry to focus attention on them.
- Make sure that things are packed and ready for the trip to the hospital or birth center. Find the car keys, but don't rush off yet. Particularly with a first baby, this stage may take a long time.

FIRST STAGE OF LABOR: 3 TO 4 CM DILATION

WHAT'S HAPPENING

The contractions have become stronger and more regular. They are becoming increasingly uncomfortable.

REACTIONS OF MOTHER

As the contractions increase in intensity, many women don't feel much like talking anymore. They become thoughtful and quiet. Although generally preoccupied with the labor and with self, most women need to know that someone is with them. Companionship rather than conversation is needed at this time. Talking during contractions is avoided. Although many women don't feel like walking, some still find it helpful.

WHAT TO DO

- Try to relax in a comfortable position. Do whatever works best for you. Some women prefer to lie down. Others are more comfortable sitting or propped up with pillows. Still others want to walk about.
- Change your position, whatever it is, at least for a short while every hour or so. Moving will help your circulation and you may even find a position you like better.
- Rest between contractions.
- If you're hungry, continue to snack lightly. Maintain your energy level and fluid intake.
- Urinate, if you can, every one to two hours during labor.
- Follow your own instincts. Don't be afraid to do what makes sense for you.

HINTS FOR HELPING

- Help promote a relaxed, quiet environment. Avoid bright lights, unnecessary noise, or commotion in the room.
- Provide encouragement and reassurance, but give her space if she wants it.

- Continue to encourage fluid intake so that she won't become dehydrated.
- Your prenatal care provider probably has given you guidelines for when to call. If this is the time, see that it's done. It's best if the person in labor talks to the caregiver directly.

FIRST STAGE OF LABOR: 5 TO 8 CM DILATION

WHAT'S HAPPENING

Contractions are more frequent now. The peak of a contraction will be reached more quickly and it lasts longer. At this point, most laboring women are in contact with their care provider and are in their chosen birth setting.

REACTIONS OF MOTHER

As labor reaches this stage, most women are very serious. Doubts about the ability to cope with the contractions yet to come are not unusual.

WHAT TO DO

- Begin using your controlled breathing techniques if you have not already done so. Stay with the deep chest breathing as long as you can. Get as much oxygen as you can to your hardworking body.
- Be assertive if you wish. If you think you need or want something, ask for it. Follow your instincts and do what makes sense to you.
- Some women may request medication to aid relaxation at this time.

HINTS FOR HELPING

- Offer words of encouragement. Things may be getting tougher to handle.
- Coach her on the controlled breathing through each contraction. If the two of you find something that works better, that's all right, too.
- Offer to supply pressure on her back to relieve backache.

FIRST STAGE OF LABOR: 8 TO 10 CM DILATION (TRANSITION)

WHAT'S HAPPENING

Very pronounced contractions are coming on quickly, one after another. Many women may find that these contractions feel continuous. There may be drowsiness between them. The abdominal wall is tense, and many women feel unable to relax. Hiccups or belching and a feeling of nausea or desire to vomit are not uncommon during this stage. Some women feel hot, others feel cold. The legs may tremble and feelings of restlessness persist. Many women have beads of perspiration on their brow or upper lip.

REACTIONS OF MOTHER

Most women at this time are extremely sensitive and irritable. They may be short-tempered and snap at people. Many women are surprised by the strength of the contractions at this stage. Their inability to relax frightens and frustrates them. This is a time that some women experience a feeling of panic and temporarily lose control. Expressions of discouragement and requests for help are frequent during this stage of labor.

WHAT TO DO

- Remember that this is the toughest part of labor for most women. It doesn't last very long, even though it may seem eternal at the time.
- Keep your eyes open during the contractions. Look at the focal point you selected and concentrate.
- Think of one contraction at a time. Look forward to a rest, however brief, after it.
- Try shallow chest breathing for this stage.
- A cool, damp cloth for the face and neck might help.
- If your mouth is dry, something wet—a damp cloth or ice chips—may help. Try a Popsicle if that appeals to you.
- Changes in position occasionally help during transition. Follow your instincts. If you can think of a way to get more comfortable, try it.

HINTS FOR HELPING

- Provide constant reassurance that the feelings of getting out of control at this stage are normal reactions to the intensity of the contractions.
- Guide her through each contraction. As you talk her through it, be firm and encouraging. Direct her in her breathing.
- Remind her that this stage is short. It will end.
- Remind her to think of just one contraction at a time. Get through this one. Don't worry about the next.
- Remind her to rest between contractions.
- Offer something cool and wet (ice chips or a Popsicle) for dry mouth.
- Wipe her face and neck with a cool washcloth.
- Look into her eyes and tell her everything will be fine. Believe it.

FIRST STAGE OF LABOR: AS TRANSITION NEARS ITS END _____

WHAT'S HAPPENING

As the transition stage nears its close, pain in the lower back probably will increase. It will be more difficult to continue the shallow chest breathing and the urge to push may become strong.

REACTIONS OF MOTHER

At this time, many women feel a conflict between the need to continue chest breathing and the need to begin pushing. This confusion is quite common.

WHAT TO DO

- Try to listen carefully to instructions from your labor coach, even though it may be difficult at this time.
- Continue shallow chest breathing with blowing until you are instructed to push or until the urge to push becomes so strong that you can't contain it.
- Tell your birth attendants of your urge to push.
- Try pressure on the lower back to relieve backache.

HINTS FOR HELPING

- Remind her not to push until it's time.
- Apply pressure on the lower back to ease her backache.
- Continue to direct controlled breathing.

SECOND STAGE OF LABOR: PUSHING AND EXPULSION

WHAT'S HAPPENING

There may be a very brief period of deep sleep as this stage begins. The contractions may be farther apart than they were during the transition stage of labor. These contractions, which will push the baby through the birth canal, require great effort on the part of the mother.

REACTIONS OF MOTHER

Many women feel an almost unbelievable sense of physical force or power at this stage. There is often surprise at the rapid change in feelings from transition to pushing. There is an irresistible urge to push, and pushing for most women brings with it relief and a sense of satisfaction. It's not uncommon for a woman at this stage to act and look as if she were having a bowel movement.

WHAT TO DO

- Ease gradually into pushing. Your natural instincts will be very strong at this time, and you should follow them with the guidance of your birth attendant.
- Try to rest completely between contractions.
- You should be able to assume whatever position you find most comfortable and effective at this time. The more traditional position of flat on the back with the legs extended may be the least efficient of all. Squatting, standing, or sitting makes

gravity your helper. Lying on your side may work well for you. Some birth centers have a birthing chair available, although it's possible to do well in a sitting or squatting position without special furniture. Your partner should feel free to support you in any position that works for you.

- Don't be afraid of your intense feelings or feel embarrassed by them. Feelings of power and pleasure are normal at this time. Enjoy them if you can.

HINTS FOR HELPING

- Reassure her that her feelings are normal and acceptable.
- Provide guidance through each contraction. Remind her to rest between them.
- The similarity of this stage of labor to having a bowel movement may embarrass some women. If she is afraid to push because she is worried about making a mess, remind her that these feelings are normal and that no harm will come from any mess that might be made.
- Support her in whatever laboring position she finds comfortable and effective. Let her hold on to you as she squats on the floor or on the bed. If she is lying on her side, try supporting her upper leg. Don't be afraid to help her find a position that works.
- Help her to focus on accomplishing her goal.

SECOND STAGE OF LABOR: FROM CROWNING TO BIRTH _____

WHAT'S HAPPENING

In a normal presentation, the baby's head is visible first. Crowning is the term used to describe the time when the head bulges the perineum and does not move back from sight between pushing contractions. If you are going to have an episiotomy (incision in the perineum to enlarge the birth opening), it will be done at this time. The head is born first, then the shoulders. After the shoulders are delivered, the rest of the baby slides out easily.

REACTIONS OF MOTHER

Most women at this time are totally absorbed in the job at hand. They are indifferent to anything else going on. Many are impatient. There is a strong desire to push. Most women become more alert and eager to see the baby. Some women, however, are overpowered by the pressure and discomfort at this time and become fearful. If this should happen to you, rely on the guidance and support of your birth attendant.

WHAT TO DO

- Work with your birth attendant. As you follow your own instincts, communicate how you feel so you can receive the best guidance for you.

- Let the birth attendant guide you in your pushing efforts. Easing the baby's head and shoulders out may help avoid unnecessary tearing. If you wish to avoid an episiotomy, patience and extra care at this time are essential.
- You may still maintain whatever position is working for you. If you are in a setting that requires that you be moved to a delivery room, the traditional table probably can be adjusted to support you in a position somewhat akin to sitting or squatting if you wish.

HINTS FOR HELPING

- If birth is to take place in a delivery room, the mother will be moved at the beginning of this stage of labor. It's easier if she is permitted to move onto the delivery table between contractions. Help her communicate her wishes so that the table is adjusted for maximum ease of delivery for her. Continue to support her as she wishes.
- Encourage cooperation with the birth attendant. Pushing as guided can make things easier.

THIRD STAGE OF LABOR: DELIVERY OF THE PLACENTA

WHAT'S HAPPENING

The contractions may stop temporarily after the baby is born. When they resume, they usually are painless. There may be a trickle or a gush of blood. Expulsion of the placenta follows. A feeling of pressure, but little or no pain, is experienced.

REACTIONS OF MOTHER

At this point, a woman is likely to be proud of her achievement. Some women feel a burst of energy and are eager to see the baby. Most women are exhausted. Many are extremely hungry and thirsty. There is no "right" way to feel. A wide range of reactions can be expected.

WHAT TO DO

- Your birth attendant will assist you as needed at this stage.
- If you had an episiotomy, it will be repaired at this time. If you didn't have an episiotomy, tears (if any) will be repaired as needed.
- Unless your baby requires urgent medical attention, he or she will be placed on your abdomen so you can begin bonding while any necessary repairs are being done.
- Many mothers choose to nurse the baby at this time.

HINTS FOR HELPING

- Share the moment.
- If you have followed Leboyer's methods for a gentle birth, you will give the baby a warm bath at this time.

BABY CARE (DELIVERY ROOM)

As soon as a baby is born, he or she must make the transition from being totally dependent on the mother to functioning independently. Your birth attendants will assist the baby, as needed, to make this transition. If the baby is having trouble breathing, helping him or her to breathe is a top priority. Mucus will be suctioned from the baby's breathing passages if necessary.

At birth, and again when the baby is five minutes old, his or her condition will be rated in five areas on a scale of 0 to 2. This rating, named for Dr. Virginia Apgar, the physician who developed it, is known as the Apgar Scale. A score of 7 or more indicates that the baby is in good condition. Most babies score 7 or higher by the five-minute check. Immediate intervention is required for a baby who scores 4 or less. The Apgar rating is an indication of how well a baby has come through the stress of labor and delivery and is not a predictor of long-term health.

Apgar Scale

Item Tested	0	1 point	2 points
Heart Rate	absent	slow (less than 100 beats per minute)	100 beats or more per minute
Breathing	absent	slow or irregular	regular
Muscle Tone	limp	some motion of extremities	active motion
Skin Color	blue	pink body, blue extremities	pink all over
Reflex Response	absent	grimace	cry

Because a mother's body temperature—which is what the newborn has been used to—is significantly higher than the temperature of the room, the baby must be kept warm. For warmth, the baby may be placed on your abdomen and a blanket used to cover you both. This way the two of you can continue to be close to each other while the placenta is delivered and the episiotomy, if you had one, is repaired.

To complete the baby's adjustment to life outside the mother, the umbilical cord must be cut. Some birth attendants prefer to clamp and cut the cord immediately after the baby is delivered. Others will wait until the cord has stopped pulsating before cutting it, unless there is some specific medical indication for doing this sooner in a particular case. When to cut the cord may be a negotiable item. If you have a preference, discuss it in advance with your caregiver.

If you plan to breastfeed, you may wish to offer your baby the breast while you are still in the delivery room or birthing room. The baby's sucking will stimulate the uterus to contract and help it to return to its normal size more quickly. If you would like to nurse your baby immediately after delivery, discuss this with your prenatal care provider. A few hospitals still discourage nursing in the delivery room because it may be inconvenient for the staff or interfere with routine procedures. It's important to make your wishes known in advance.

If you are following Leboyer's procedures for a gentle birth, your baby will receive a warm bath soon after delivery. Some couples choose to use the bath as one means to involve the father in the baby's care right from the start.

Before you and your baby leave the delivery room or birthing room, a record will be made of your baby's footprints along with one or more of your fingerprints. Your baby will get identification bracelets—one on an ankle and one on a wrist. You will receive an identical bracelet for your own wrist. The purpose of these procedures is, of course, to make sure that your baby is not mixed up with anyone else's child.

ADDITIONAL MEDICAL PROCEDURES _____

In most states, the law requires that newborn babies be given medication in their eyes to prevent infection. In many places, antibiotic ointment is now used for this purpose in preference to the more irritating silver nitrate drops. Many birth attendants are willing to delay administration of any medication until after the parents have had a chance to hold their newborn and enjoy eye contact with the baby as part of the bonding process. Discuss with your caregiver in advance what eye medication will be used for your baby and when it will be administered. If you expect to be allowed to have time with your baby before routine medical procedures are administered, be sure to communicate your wishes to your care provider.

In most hospitals, babies receive an injection of vitamin K to help the blood in clotting. Some hospitals routinely administer penicillin to all newborns to help prevent them from contracting an infection in the hospital nursery. Treatment would also be indicated in cases where maternal infection might be transmitted to the newborn in the birth canal. The baby's blood might be tested for PKU disease, a rare form of mental retardation that can be prevented if detected and treated early. Many pediatricians routinely order the baby's blood to be tested for bilirubin level.

During your pregnancy, you should feel free to discuss with your prenatal care provider the routine procedures that your new baby would be likely to encounter in your chosen birth setting. If you have any questions about such procedures as they are happening, don't be afraid to ask.

BABY CARE (NURSERY) _____

In the hospital or birth center, your baby will be watched closely to make sure that all systems are working well. Because a newborn may have difficulty regulating his or her own body temperature at first, a heated bed may be used for a while until the baby's body temperature is normal. Don't be afraid to ask about the procedures that are being followed for your baby.

At most hospitals, a baby will be brought to his or her mother whenever the baby seems hungry. If your baby is sharing your room (rooming in) rather than staying in the nursery, he or she will already be right there whenever it's feeding time. As a general rule, mothers are encouraged to feed their babies at least every four hours and to allow two hours to pass between feedings if possible. This is true for bottle-fed as well as breastfed infants. Individual circumstances, however, may vary.

If you are breastfeeding your baby and prefer not to have bottles of glucose and water offered to your child in the nursery, you should discuss this in advance with your baby's care provider. He or she will make the appropriate notation on the baby's chart. Follow the same procedure if you do not want your baby to be given a pacifier in the nursery.

CIRCUMCISION

If your baby is a boy, one of the earliest decisions you will have to make is whether or not to have him circumcised. Because circumcision has been such a widespread practice in this country, many parents are under the impression it is a necessity. They mistakenly believe they must agree to have it done. This is simply not so. There is no compelling medical reason for routine circumcision. Regular bathing can prevent the same problems that circumcision prevents.

Whether or not to have your child circumcised is a personal choice. Circumcision of the newborn has routinely been performed without anesthesia. Babies do feel pain, however, and some practitioners are now willing to use a local anesthetic for the procedure. Because the risks involved in use of a local anesthetic may outweigh the benefits to the baby, this is a matter you may wish to discuss with your care provider so that you can make an informed decision.

It's generally best to delay circumcision for at least twenty-four hours after the baby is born. Jewish ritual circumcision is done on the eighth day.

NAMING YOUR BABY

Soon after your baby is born, someone from the hospital or birth center staff will contact you to obtain information for the baby's birth certificate. If you have not yet decided on a name, you may leave the space for the name blank. Depending on the state in which you live, you have from ten days to seven years to record the child's name. Once a name is recorded on the birth certificate, however, it may take a court order to change it.

While many parents choose to have their child use the father's last name, some do not. Especially when the woman has kept her own surname in marriage, parents may prefer to have the child use a hyphenated combination of the mother's name and the father's name. Sometimes parents create a new surname using elements of both family names. A child of unmarried parents often uses the mother's surname, but this is not required. A child's surname need not be that of either parent as long as no fraud is intended.

If you are planning to do something untraditional or unusual with your child's name, check ahead of time to find out what special regulations, if any, there are in the state in which you live. If you prefer not to name your baby in a traditional way, don't be intimidated by those who insist you must. Make sure the official records reflect your wishes.

YOUR CARE (AFTER DELIVERY) _____

After your baby is born, especially for the first few hours, you will be watched very carefully. Your blood pressure reading will probably be taken several times and your uterus will be checked frequently to see if it is remaining firm.

Beginning right after delivery, you will experience a vaginal flow known as lochia. This is a normal process of cleansing and will continue until the place where the placenta was attached to the uterus has healed. The flow will occur if you had a Caesarean delivery as well as if you delivered vaginally. Lochia begins as a heavy flow similar in appearance to menstrual blood. It may contain clots. Your vaginal flow will be monitored to make sure it is not excessive. Tell your caregiver if your flow soaks through two pads in less than thirty minutes or if you pass a clot larger than a lemon.

Many women are exhausted after delivery and are content to rest. Others, however, experience intense feelings of exhilaration and find sleep temporarily inappropriate. Those around you should try to understand and respect your personal response to the birthing experience.

If you are hungry after delivery, as many women tend to be, don't be afraid to ask for something even if it's not time for a regularly scheduled meal.

HOSPITAL STAY _____

The length of time you stay in the hospital or birth center will be determined by many factors: your condition and that of your baby, your personal preferences, and the practices generally followed by your birth attendant, your baby's caregiver, your insurance carrier, and the hospital or birth center in which you deliver. The trend today is toward shorter stays in cases where delivery was routine for both mother and baby. Many women are now leaving the hospital a day or two after delivery, with some choosing to leave less than twenty-four hours after the baby is born. Some birth centers are set up to encourage discharge shortly after a typical delivery. A short stay costs less than a longer one, and many parents find adjusting to their new baby easier in the familiar setting of home. Others, however, may welcome the opportunity to enjoy the change of pace they find in a hospital setting for a day or two longer.

If you have a Caesarean delivery, your stay in the hospital will probably be somewhat longer than it would have been with a routine vaginal delivery. The average stay after a Caesarean is five days, although you may be able to leave sooner.

Recently, some families and care providers have become concerned that the economic pressure for early discharge from the birth setting can force care choices that may not be in the best interests of a woman and/or her newborn. In response, a number of states have passed legislation requiring that insurance carriers cover a minimum postpartum stay of 48 hours for a routine delivery, and longer for a Caesarean.

Discuss with your prenatal care provider the likely duration of your stay in the hospital or birth center. Find out what you will be permitted to do if all goes well. Remember, however, that medical reasons may develop to keep you in the hospital longer than you would like, regardless of what arrangements were made in advance.

Be sure to discuss with your care provider any concerns you may have, especially if you leave the birth setting soon after delivery, whether by choice or because of economic or other reasons. Home health care by a trained practitioner such as a visiting nurse may be an option available to you if need additional assistance. Ask whatever questions you may have, and be sure you are comfortable with the answers before you're on your own.

SECTION SIX

POSTPARTUM CARE

POSTPARTUM CARE _____

The following pages contain information on topics related to your own care after giving birth. Try to read these carefully before you leave the hospital or birth center so you can discuss any questions you might have with your care provider. There is space on page 147 to note any special instructions for your particular situation.

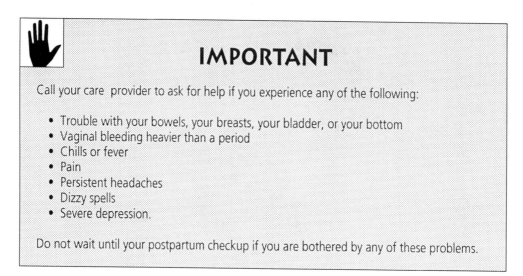

IMPORTANT

Call your care provider to ask for help if you experience any of the following:

- Trouble with your bowels, your breasts, your bladder, or your bottom
- Vaginal bleeding heavier than a period
- Chills or fever
- Pain
- Persistent headaches
- Dizzy spells
- Severe depression.

Do not wait until your postpartum checkup if you are bothered by any of these problems.

ACTIVITIES _____

Common sense is an important ingredient in planning your activities during the first few weeks after your baby is born. If something seems to be a strain, skip it until you're better able. If you can get help with household chores, that's great. If you can't, leave everything except the absolute essentials. Forget about rearranging furniture or cleaning closets for a while.

Walk up and down stairs when necessary, but you probably shouldn't carry anything heavier than your baby for the first week or two. If you have older children who want to be held, you can sit down and let them climb onto your lap rather than lifting them.

Most women are quite able to drive a car and run short errands when they first get home after delivery. If you find yourself spending a lot of time doing such things, however, you're probably not resting as much as you should be.

Rest (see page 148) is an essential part of your postpartum care. A safe and comfortable level of activity for you at first will depend on several factors, including how fit you were before and during your pregnancy, how difficult your delivery was, and any complications you might have experienced. While some women may feel able to jog, play tennis, ride a horse, or resume aerobics classes a fortnight or so after delivery, most do not and should not.

Before leaving the hospital or birth center, you should discuss with your care provider your plans for getting back to your normal activities. Find out which activities are fine for you right away and which should wait until after your postpartum checkup.

AFTERBIRTH PAINS

During pregnancy, the uterus increases greatly in size. Right after delivery, it will be about the size of a grapefruit. It will continue to get smaller each day until it has returned to its normal size. This process, called involution, takes about four to six weeks.

As your uterus contracts after delivery, you may experience cramps that are sometimes referred to as "afterpains" or "afterbirth pains." These contractions may cause some discomfort for two or three days. You will be more likely to notice afterpains if this is not your first baby. This is because your uterus will have to work harder to return to its prepregnancy condition with subsequent pregnancies than it did the first time around.

Breastfeeding stimulates contractions that help return the uterus to its normal size. If you are nursing your baby, you will be more likely to notice the afterbirth contractions in the first few days after delivery. If you find the afterpains bothersome, gentle massage or lying face down with a pillow under your abdomen may help. If the cramps are very severe, consult your care provider, who may prescribe something for the pain. If you do take something, it's important that it be safe for your nursing baby.

BATHING

You are likely to feel better if you keep your body as clean as possible after delivery. While you are still in the hospital or birth center, you probably will be encouraged to take a daily shower. Warm, shallow baths (sitz baths) will ease soreness from hemorrhoids and episiotomy repair.

Some care providers advise that a woman avoid deep tub baths for three or four weeks after delivery to make sure water doesn't enter unhealed body cavities. Others feel that problems are so unlikely that such restrictions are not needed. If you prefer baths to showers, ask if any special circumstances of your case might make a tub bath unwise.

After delivery, the body has its own natural cleansing process to rid you of waste blood, mucus, and other tissue. Your vaginal discharge at this time is a natural occurrence. Douching is unnecessary and may be inadvisable. Most caregivers recommend that a woman not douche until after her postpartum checkup.

BREAST CARE (IF BOTTLE-FEEDING)

If you are bottle-feeding, you may be given medication to help dry up your milk supply. For a few days after delivery, your breasts may feel uncomfortable. If your breasts are engorged (swollen and full), apply an ice pack. An over-the-counter pain reliever may help. Ask your care provider for suggestions about what to take.

Wear a comfortably tight bra with good support. Keep your breasts clean and dry. If you are not breastfeeding your baby, avoid the temptation to express milk to relieve the fullness of engorged breasts. Expressing milk will stimulate your body to produce more. Restricting your fluid intake for a few days may be helpful.

BREAST CARE (IF BREASTFEEDING)

If you are breastfeeding your baby, use only warm water to keep your breasts clean. Avoid soap, which tends to dry out the nipples and cause them to crack. Be sure that your nursing bras are the right size and that they provide good support.

If your breasts are sore, you may find these suggestions helpful:

- Try shorter feedings more often. Express a little milk before putting the baby to the breast to get the flow started.
- Put the baby to the less sore breast first. Vary the nursing position to avoid putting the most pressure on the same part of the nipple each time.
- For dry, cracked nipples, use lanolin or one of the commercially available creams especially formulated for this purpose.
- Let your nipples dry in warm air after a feeding. Leave them exposed when you can. Absorbent pads to protect your clothes are helpful, but avoid the types of breast shields that trap moisture close to the skin, because this may add to the irritation.

Many new mothers find that their breasts become engorged when their milk supply first comes in, around the third or fourth day after delivery. Feeding more frequently will help, while delaying a feeding because of feared pain will only make matters worse. Either heat or cold might help. Some women take comfort in a hot shower. Others find that an ice pack works well. You can easily make cold compress by wrapping a few ice cubes in a diaper.

If your breasts become red and painfully tender in spots, consult your care provider. If you have a fever, it's especially important to get treatment before a developing infection gets out of hand. Shoulder rotation exercises (see page 71) may help some by enhancing circulation to the breast area.

If you are nursing your baby and are having difficulty, a volunteer from La Leche League may be able to give you the support and encouragement you need to get beyond the early problems so you can nurse successfully. Your care provider (or your baby's) can probably direct you to volunteers in your area. If not, you can contact the La Leche League headquarters directly at (708) 445-7730. The toll-free number, (800) LA LECHE, is staffed part time, and a recording will direct you to emergency assistance at any other time. The address is: La Leche League International, 9616 Minneapolis Avenue, Franklin Park, Ill. 60131.

CAESAREAN POSTPARTUM

If you deliver your baby by Caesarean section, it probably will take you a bit longer to resume full activity than it might have otherwise. Remember, you have to recover from major surgery as well as cope with your newborn. A woman who delivers by Caesarean has a greater blood loss than one who delivers vaginally and may need to be treated for anemia, which could prolong the convalescence somewhat.

After a Caesarean delivery, you will be encouraged to get up and move around as soon as possible. Even if you don't feel like doing it, walking will improve your circulation, help prevent blood clots, reduce intestinal swelling, and promote healing. Being in an upright position may help ease the intestinal gas pains that sometimes follow a Caesarean delivery.

The exercises to strengthen your abdominal muscles (see pages 72–73) are very useful after a Caesarean. Ask your care provider when it is safe for you to begin these exercises. Begin slowly and increase the time very gradually. Stop if you feel pain or severe discomfort.

CONSTIPATION

Constipation is sometimes a problem for a new mother. Be sure your diet includes sufficient quantities of fluids and fiber. Whole grains and fresh fruits and vegetables are your best dietary sources of natural fiber. Maintain the sound nutrition plan suggested for you before your baby's birth (see pages 37–67). Walking (gently at first, and then briskly as you become able) will aid your digestion and circulation.

If you have soreness from an episiotomy or hemorrhoids, you may be afraid of trying to have a bowel movement. This fear can add to your problems. Try to relax. Reread the suggestions (see page 24) for dealing with constipation during pregnancy. These suggestions are still valid.

If constipation is a problem for you, consult your care provider. A stool softener or a laxative may be suggested if dietary measures seem to be temporarily insufficient.

DEPRESSION (POSTPARTUM BLUES)

You've probably heard people talk about the postpartum blues or baby blues, a condition many women experience a short time after giving birth. If this seemingly uncontrollable feeling of unhappiness hits you, don't panic. No matter how delighted you are with your baby, it's possible and even normal to feel like crying for a few days. There are physiological reasons why this can happen.

Feelings of depression often accompany the body's attempt to regain its fluid-salt balance after giving birth. For most women, this balance returns four to seven days after delivery. For some, it may take as long as ten days. Hormonal changes may contribute to postpartum mood swings. Interrupted sleep patterns may also influence the way a woman feels and copes.

In addition to physiological factors, which readily explain most cases of postpartum blues, there may be emotional stresses as well. New motherhood will involve adjustments in a woman's relationship with her baby, her mate, and other family members. For some, the intensity of the birthing experience and the exhilaration of having a new baby will be tempered by an overwhelming sense of the responsibilities involved. Anxiety and feelings of self-doubt are not unusual. All of these experiences occur while a new mother has not yet rebounded from the extraordinary physical exertion of labor and delivery.

What can you expect in the days and weeks right after your baby is born? It's probably wise to hope for the best and take one day at a time. Don't plan on being depressed, because you shouldn't set up a self-fulfilling prophecy. It's entirely possible that you will not experience any significant degree of postpartum depression. Many women don't. If you do find yourself overwhelmed to tears, however, by your body's physiological changes and/or the emotional stresses of new motherhood, realize that a number of women have such feelings. You are not alone.

What should you do if you are hit by the baby blues? Don't be afraid to tell your mate and your caregiver how you feel. Try to minimize physical stress by getting as much rest as you can. Ask for help in the house and with your baby if you need it. Try to get a little uninterrupted time for yourself. Get someone to stay with your baby long enough for you to take a walk, a nap, or a long bath, or to visit with a friend without being interrupted.

Chances are your feelings of depression will pass within a few days. If you feel overwhelmed by depression much beyond the first ten days to two weeks, however, ask your care provider for guidance. If you become seriously unable to communicate with those you love or to care for yourself and your baby, you may need professional help in addition to rest and time.

EPISIOTOMY AFTERCARE

If you had an episiotomy or sutures to repair tearing, the stitches may itch or feel sore at first. Here are some suggestions:

- An ice pack, especially in the first twenty-four hours, may be helpful to reduce the swelling.
- Try warm water. Sit in a warm, shallow bath (sitz bath) or let the water from your shower run over your perineum. Warm water stimulates circulation and will promote healing while soothing discomfort.
- A number of creams, sprays, and foams with local anesthetic are available. Apply one to your sanitary pad.
- When you sit, avoid putting direct presure on the perineum at first. You'll probably feel more comfortable sitting on something soft. Carry a small pillow with you and use it wherever you need to.
- As you urinate, pour some warm water over your perineum to ease any burning or stinging sensation.
- Begin doing Kegel exercises (see page 68), even if it hurts at first. The exercises will help promote healing by stimulating circulation in the perineal area.

A positive attitude is perhaps the most helpful of all. If you fear moving about because you think it might hurt too much, it probably will. Don't dwell on the discomfort. Pretend it doesn't hurt when you do your exercises and walk around. Soon it won't.

If, instead of symptoms subsiding, your perineum becomes further reddened or swollen, or if pain (rather than discomfort) persists, consult your care provider. These problems may signal complications and should be checked out.

EXERCISE

Many of the exercises described on pages 68–74 are useful after delivery to help you regain your muscle tone and energy. You probably will be able to begin doing Kegel exercises and the exercises for separated abdominal muscles almost immediately. How rapidly you will be able to embark on a more strenuous exercise program and resume your normal activities such as sports, however, will depend on a number of factors. These include your fitness before delivery, any complications you might have had, your own motivation, and your body's ability to bounce back. You should discuss your intended activities with your care provider and, above all, use common sense. If it doesn't feel right, don't do it yet.

FAMILY PLANNING

The method of family planning you use should be a personal choice based on what is recommended as medically safe and effective for you as well as what you find comfortable and consistent with your beliefs.

If you have just had a baby, here are some facts about family planning you should keep in mind.

- After pregnancy, it is possible for a woman to ovulate before having a menstrual period. In other words, you can become pregnant again soon after your baby's birth even if you have not yet had a menstrual period.
- Although some nursing mothers do not ovulate as long as they are breastfeeding, others do. Breastfeeding is not a reliable method of birth control.
- If your choice of family-planning method is the diaphragm, the one that worked for you in the past probably does not fit. You can be measured for a new one at your postpartum checkup.
- Do not use oral contraceptives (birth control pills) if you are breastfeeding without first consulting your care provider. Oral contraceptives may decrease your milk supply, and the hormones from them can be transmitted to the baby in the milk.
- If you wish to use an IUD, it can be inserted once your uterus has returned to its normal size. Ask your care provider about this at your postpartum checkup.
- If natural family planning is your family-planning technique of choice, remember that it may take some time for your menstrual cycle to regulate itself after childbirth. When your cycle does reestablish itself, it may be slightly different from what it was previous to your pregnancy.
- If you plan to get an IUD or a diaphragm at your postpartum checkup but resume sexual relations sooner, consider using condoms, contraceptive foam, or contraceptive jelly during this interim time.

HEMORRHOIDS

Many women have a problem with hemorrhoids after delivery. Constipation, which also troubles many women after delivery, can make hemorrhoids even worse. The suggestions for easing discomfort caused by hemorrhoids during pregnancy (see page 28) will help now as well. If your hemorrhoids are especially painful and you feel that you need medication, consult your care provider. Self-medication may be unwise, especially if you are breastfeeding.

LOCHIA

Lochia is the vaginal flow that begins right after delivery and continues until the place where the placenta was attached to the uterus has healed. For most women, the discharge lasts about four to six weeks. Lochia is the body's normal cleansing process after childbirth.

Lochia begins as a heavy flow similar in appearance to menstrual blood. At first, it is likely to contain clots, some of them quite large. The flow then turns brown, and then yellowish white or colorless before stopping completely.

Use sanitary pads, not tampons, and change them frequently. The pads provided in the hospital or birth center will be individually wrapped in sterile packages, a useful precaution for the first few days after delivery.

Keep yourself clean. Irrigate the perineum and outer vaginal area with warm water. The hospital or birth center may give you a squeeze bottle for this purpose. (If so, you can use it for plants when you no longer need it for you.) If not, you can splash warm water onto yourself from a clean paper cup. Wipe yourself gently from front to back, and use each tissue only once.

Lochia may be a very heavy flow, especially at first. How heavy is too heavy? If you soak through two pads in half an hour or pass a clot larger than a lemon, report this to your caregiver. You should also note changes in color of the discharge. Normal sequence is from red to brown to pale yellowish white or colorless before ceasing altogether. If your flow should turn from brown back to bright red, however, you should inform your caregiver if the condition persists. This may be a sign that you have exerted yourself too much and temporarily interrupted the healing process.

LOVEMAKING

How soon after delivery can a couple have intercourse? There are no absolute answers to this question. It's probably best to wait three or four weeks to allow the vaginal wall muscles to regain their strength and the episiotomy, if any, to heal. Ask your care provider whether or not there are special circumstances in your case that might make waiting longer than this advisable. Some caregivers advise that a woman wait until after her postpartum checkup to resume having intercourse.

You may feel a bit uncomfortable at first, because tissues are still tender. Talk to your partner about this. A slight change in position or a little extra gentleness may help. A lubricant such as K-Y jelly may be helpful. Don't worry. Discomfort, if any, is a very temporary condition. It will pass.

If you are breastfeeding your baby, you might find that your breasts leak during intercourse. Don't be concerned. This slight flow of milk is a normal response to sexual excitement.

Remember that you could become pregnant again very soon after delivery unless you take specific precautions not to. Even if you have not had a menstrual period, you may have ovulated. Breastfeeding is not a means of contraception. It is possible to become pregnant while breastfeeding an infant.

It's best to discuss with your care provider what you will do about family planning before the need is urgent. This is a matter you would do well to consider before delivery, so you will be prepared when you need to be. (See "Family Planning," page 145.)

POSTPARTUM CHECKUP

Your first postpartum checkup is a very important one. The exact timing of this checkup, which will probably be four to six weeks after your baby is born, will vary according to your caregiver's general policies and your specific needs. You may be seen sooner after a Caesarean delivery.

At your postpartum checkup, you will be examined to make sure that your uterus has returned to its normal size and position and that your episiotomy, if you had one, has healed. A Pap smear and breast examination may be done as well. This is the time to ask your care provider any questions you still have about diet, vitamins, exercise, family planning, and any other matters related to your personal health care and childbearing.

Although your care provider expects you for a postpartum checkup, it's still up to you to make the appointment. Call the office to reserve a time as soon as you can after delivery. Use the space that follows to note the details of your appointment and any particular questions you want to ask.

POSTPARTUM CHECKUP
Date: _____   Time: _____
Caregiver: _____

REST

After you have had a baby, you may be extremely tired. Fatigue is a normal postpartum occurrence. Your body has been under severe stress, and you need time to recover.

Rest whenever you can. When your baby sleeps, you should, too, although this may be impossible if you have other young children. Common sense is the rule here. Don't take on unnecessary tasks until you are able. The house can do without cleaning for a while. You need not entertain or put your baby on display for acquaintances whose company drains your energy.

If you can afford household help, get someone to do cleaning chores and laundry. The hired help should do the tasks that are drudgery. This will enable you to use what energy you have to take care of and enjoy your baby. When family or friends make demands you are too tired to meet, remind them that your caregiver has ordered you to rest. You'll never have a better excuse than you do now.

If an iron supplement has been prescribed, be sure to take it. In the days after delivery, anemia is a common cause of fatigue. Give your care provider a call if you are feeling extremely tired and a reasonable amount of rest doesn't seem to be helping.

WEIGHT LOSS

If your weight gain during pregnancy was within the recommended range and from nutritious foods, you should be able to lose much or even all of it within the first two months. Don't be disappointed, however, if it takes at least that long. Many women, particularly first-time mothers, are surprised to find they didn't come out of the delivery room slim and ready for their prepregnancy wardrobe.

During delivery, you will shed the weight of your baby, the placenta, and the amniotic fluid (see page 114). The rest of your pregnancy weight gain will take a little longer, although you can probably get rid of much of the excess fluid within the first week or two. It will take at least another month to lose the extra weight of your enlarged uterus and other tissue.

Do not go on a crash diet right after your baby is born, no matter how motivated you might be to strive for thinness. You need nutritious food to regain your strength, to promote healing, and to give you enough energy to care for your baby. Continue to follow the basic principles depicted in the Food Guide Pyramid (see pages 38–43). Stay away from food fads and diet pills. You need a balanced diet.

Continue the prenatal vitamins and iron supplement you were taking during pregnancy, unless your care provider directs otherwise. If you are breastfeeding, you may require up to one thousand additional calories of nutritious fluids and foods daily.

If you are maintaining a well-planned program of nutritious meals and adequate exercise and your weight loss is still slower than you think it should be, discuss this with your care provider.

INDEX

Special Discount Offer to While Waiting readers!

Order **Welcome Baby** (86121-4) and **Talk and Toddle** (78430-9) and save $3.00! Complete your library of Anne Mueser Infant-care books today and take $3.00 off the regular delivered price.

Enclosed is $10.90 (includes postage). Please send me one copy each of **Welcome Baby** and **Talk and Toddle**.

Name _____

Address _____

City/State/Zip _____

Send this form with payment to: St. Martin's Press, Cash Sales Department, 175 Fifth Avenue, New York, N.Y. 10010.

This offer is good while stock lasts. Please allow three weeks for delivery.

Additional copies of **While Waiting** or any of the St. Martin's Press perinatal care books recommended on pages 117–120 may be purchased from most booksellers or by mail on the order form below. Substantial discounts on orders of ten or more books are available to physicians, clinics, midwives, childbirth educators, and organizations. To place an order, call St. Martin's Order Taking Department toll-free at (800) 221-7945, ext. 346, 537, or 789.

Order Form

Book	Copies	Price
While Waiting ($6.95) ISBN: 0-312-09938-X		
Mientras Espera ($7.95) ISBN: 0-312-11027-8		
Welcome Baby: A Guide to the First Six Weeks ($6.95) ISBN: 0-312-86121-4		
Talk and Toddle: A Commonsense Guide for the First Three Years ($7.95) ISBN: 0-312-78430-9		
Babysense: A Practical and Supportive Guide to Baby Care ($16.95) ISBN: 0-312-05056-9		
Beyond Jennifer and Jason: An Enlightened Guide to Naming Your Baby ($11.95) ISBN: 0-312-10426-X		
Breastfeeding and the Working Mother ($11.95) ISBN: 0-312-09527-9		
Safe & Sound: How to Prevent and Treat the Most Common Childhood Emergencies ($8.95) ISBN: 0-312-02276-X		
Homeopathy for Pregnancy, Birth, and Your Baby's First Year ($15.95) ISBN: 0-312-08809-4		
The Parent's Guide to Raising Twins ($10.95) ISBN: 0-312-03906-9		
The Premature Baby Book: A Parent's Guide to Coping and Caring in the First Years ($19.95) ISBN: 0-312-63649-0		
Twins, Triplets and More ($17.95) ISBN: 0-312-07876-5		
Yoga for Pregnancy: Safe and Gentle Stretches ($13.95) ISBN: 0-312-02322-7		

Postage and Handling
($3.00 for first book, 75¢ for each additional book)

Amount Enclosed:

Name _____

Address _____

City/State/Zip _____

Send this form with payment to: Publishers Book & Audio, P.O. Box 070059,

5448 Arthur Kill Road, Staten Island, N.Y. 10307, Telephone: (800) 288-2131. Please

allow three weeks for delivery.